R.G. Floods

December 1988.

Saddle Tramp
on the
Isle of Man

ROBERT ORRELL

ROBERT HALE · LONDON

Robert Hale Limited
Clerkenwell House
Clerkenwell Green
London EC1R 0HT

British Library Cataloguing in Publication Data

Orrell, Robert
    Saddle tramp on the Isle of Man.
    1. Isle of Man—Description and travel
    I. Title
    914.27′904858   DA670.M2

    ISBN 0-7090-3275-7

Photoset in North Wales by
Derek Doyle & Associates, Mold, Clwyd.
Printed in Great Britain by
St Edmundsbury Press Ltd, Bury St Edmunds, Suffolk.
Bound by Hunter & Foulis Ltd.

Contents

List of Illustrations

Acknowledgements

The author gratefully acknowledges the assistance of the following individuals and organizations: Captain Andrew Douglas, IOM Steam Packet Company; Staff of the Douglas Library and Museum; Harry Fancy, Whitehaven Museum; Simon Richardson, Manx Radio; Warren Elsby, Keswick Library; Jennifer Shaw, Oban; J. Barbour & Sons – waterproof clothing and saddlebags; Berghaus – climbing boots; Buffalo – sleeping bag; A.B. Optimus – paraffin stove; Pentax UK – photographic equipment; Phoenix Mountaineering – lightweight tent; Polysox – socks; Puffa Rumward – quilted jacket; Silva – compass; Troll Industries – pack-saddle bags and lightweight clothing.

The photograph of *Odin's Raven* is used by permission of Mr Robin Bigland, St John's, Isle of Man. All other photographs taken by the author.

For Jean
who gave the story a happy ending

THE OFFICE OF THE SPEAKER
LEGISLATIVE BUILDINGS
ISLE OF MAN

Foreword by
Sir Charles Kerruish, OBE, SHK, CP

I am very pleased to contribute a foreword to this book.

It is always beneficial – and sometimes a very salutory lesson – to learn how others see us. Mr Orrell's book affords the people of the Isle of Man a chance to do just that, and in a most pleasant and enjoyable way too!

I welcome this addition to the list of Manx books.

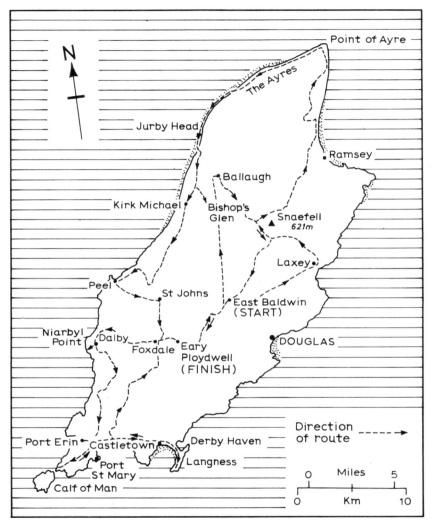

N

Point of Ayre

The Ayres

Jurby Head

Ramsey

Ballaugh

Kirk Michael

Bishop's
Glen

Snaefell
621m

Laxey

Peel

St Johns

East Baldwin
(START)

Niarbyl
Point

Dalby

Foxdale

Eary
Ploydwell
(FINISH)

DOUGLAS

Direction
of route

Port Erin

Castletown

Derby Haven

Langness

Port
St Mary

Calf of Man

Miles

0   5

0   Km   10

The Isle of Man

1

No Butter, Beer or Ponies

'I mentioned a scheme which I had of making a tour
to the Isle of Man and giving a full account of it.'
Boswell, *Life of Johnson*

'Unless you get the necessary certificates, you're not taking
those ponies across to the Isle of Man, and that's that!'

The official banged the office window shut, slumped
back heavily into his chair and bit angrily into a meat pie. A
clock on the wall ticked relentlessly towards 2 p.m. and a
ship's siren blared across the harbour, warning that the Isle
of Man ferry was about to leave. Desperately I hammered
on the window again, but the official interrupted his lunch
only to point his meat pie at a piece of paper stuck on the
window. I did not need to read it again – we had been
arguing over it for the past hour. It was an official notice
couched in the flowery language of the legal profession and
in large letters threatened dire consequences for anyone
intent on destroying the economy of the island and the
morals of its people by importing such dangerous goods as
animals, butter, meat and beer.

I had no such wicked intentions; I simply wanted to take
Thor and Lucy, my two Fell ponies, and have an enjoyable
time exploring the island. Judging by the size of print,
landing animals without permission was a far less serious
crime than importing butter, meat or beer, but there it
was: 'Animals must not be brought onto the island without
a declaration of health, and permission of the Isle of Man
Government.'

I stormed outside and ran across the quay to my
horsebox.

'Why on earth do I need permission just to take a couple
of ponies across to the island?' I fumed at the group of

11

crewmen waiting to guide my vehicle onto the ship. 'It's part of England, isn't it?' The crewmen looked at each other, but no one spoke. 'Well, isn't it?' I repeated angrily. 'The Hebrides are part of Scotland, but you don't have to put up with this sort of bureaucratic nonsense to take animals out there.'

'Mister,' said one of the crewmen, looking up from the racing page of the *Daily Mirror* and ramming the stub of a pencil behind his ear, 'Mister, if you're coming over to the island, the first thing you'll have to learn is that we're not part of England, Scotland, Wales, Ireland or any other damned country. The Isle of Man is a separate country with its own government and rules, and the sooner people realize it the better.' He turned and stalked down the ramp onto the ship.

'Don't take any notice of him,' laughed his mates. 'He's been bitten by the Nationalist bug.' One of them yelled after the departing figure, 'Tell the Mate to come up!'

An officer clutching a walkie-talkie radio came rushing out of the ship's hold. 'What's the trouble?' he panted breathlessly. 'We're about to leave and you're holding us up.'

I explained that in all the preparations for my journey no one had advised me that I needed both a vet's certificate and permission from the Isle of Man Government to land ponies on the island, and I had driven all the way from Cumberland only to find that I could not board the ship. What was I to do?

The Mate listened patiently, then spoke tersely into his radio. 'Captain, we've got a problem. There's a feller here with two ponies in a horsebox who's booked to go across to the island, and no one's told him about vet's certificates and permits. What'll we do with him?' He released the transmission button. The radio hissed and crackled, but the words were unmistakable: 'Oh, bloody hell, why does it have to happen to me?' There was a silence, then the radio crackled into life again. 'I'll give him half an hour. If he can get a vet to give the animals a certificate, I'll radio Douglas to ask permission to load them.'

I raced across to a telephone box by the booking office. 'There's a vet at Carnforth,' shouted one of the crew. I thumbed through the yellow pages and dialled his number, praying that he hadn't been called out.

'Carnforth 65 ...'

I rammed home the coin. 'Is that the vet?' I yelled.

'Yes, what can I do for you?'

I babbled out my story. Please could he come over right away?

'I'll be there in fifteen minutes,' he said, and slammed the phone down. I ran back to the horsebox and waited. Ten minutes passed, then fifteen, and there was still no sign of the vet. A dull roar of engines vibrated from the ship and black smoke poured from her funnels. On the wing of the bridge the Captain began to bellow orders. The Mate, standing by the loading ramp, looked at his watch, then at me, and shook his head despairingly.

Suddenly a car appeared, being driven at a furious rate along the quay. It screeched to a halt beside the horsebox and out leapt the vet, stethoscope round his neck and grasping a leather bag. Without saying a word he ran up the ramp of the box and proceeded to give Thor and Lucy a thorough examination. He fired a stream of questions at me about their health and, pronouncing them 'as fit as fiddles', wrote out a certificate.

'They're OK, Captain,' said the Mate into his radio.

'Get 'em aboard quickly,' came the reply, and I drove the box down the ramp into the hold of the ship. The huge steel door clanged behind us, crewmen hurriedly shackled retaining chains to the wheels of the car and trailer, and by the time I had made sure the ponies were comfortable and clambered up to the open deck, Heysham harbour was behind us and the bow of the ship was dipping gently into the grey Irish Sea. We were on our way to Douglas!

*

According to legend, the Devil liked a part of Ireland so much that he dug it up with his claws and was flying over the sea with it when he met St Patrick, who squirted some holy water at him. In his rush to dodge out of the way, Old Nick dropped his burden into the sea, where it became the Isle of Man, and it is said that, if you measure Lough Neagh and look at its general shape, it is where the Isle of

Man once was.

Scientific types, always quick to discount anything which cannot be put to the test under a microscope or thumped with a geological hammer, insist that the island is simply a lump of slate of the Upper Cambrian era, with a touch of Lower Carboniferous here and there and a slice of Red Sandstone thrown in for good measure. They even have a theory that once upon a time the island could have been connected to the mountains of Cumberland, and when the glaciers of the Ice Age had finished carving out the landscape and the last lump of ice had melted and all was quiet, there, rising out of the water, was an island thirty miles long by ten miles wide – an island destined to have an exceedingly turbulent life, yet to emerge as one of the most attractive and intriguing places in the whole of the British Isles.

There are many colourful stories told about how the island was first discovered, but a favourite tells of how a mermaid fell in love with a young man who used to come every day to tend his sheep among the rocks along the shore. She brought him presents of fine pearls and pieces of coral, 'accompanied with smiles, patting of the cheek, and all the marks of the most tender passion'. One day, though, the passion went beyond smiles and cheek-patting, and she flung her arms around him with such vigour that the poor chap thought she was trying to drag him into the sea; shouting for his mum, he ran for home. Peeved at the way he had spurned her love, the mermaid enveloped the island in a thick mist which hid it from passing ships, until one day some fishermen discovered it while sheltering from a gale and spread the word. Shiploads of adventurers set out for the island and, after a fierce fight with the natives, took control of it. After that it is said the island became an asylum for the distressed princes and great men of Europe. Encouraged by a favourable income tax rate, it seems to have been that way ever since.

Having discovered the island of their dreams, those early conquerors would be anxious to give it a name; though if they had known what confusion and disagreement they were to cause among scholars and historians centuries later, they might have taken more time over the choice of it. Explanations of the name 'Man' are as fanciful as they are numerous. Julius Caesar is said to have used the name Mona, others have called it Monabia, Monaida, Monoeda or even Menavia. During a period when the island was considered part of the Hebrides, it was known as Eubonia. One eighteenth-century writer argues that the name 'Manne' found favour because it was St Patrick's name before he changed it to Patricius, and yet another insists that it was named after Manannan MacLir, the legendary first ruler of the island. A more logical explanation of the name comes from the Celtic 'Meadhon In', (pronounced 'Mannin') meaning 'The Middle Island', though whether this meant in the middle of the Irish Sea or the middle one of three islands, i.e. England, Man and Ireland, is not clear. Out of all these evolved Ellan Vannin, the Isle of Man.

For a long time I had looked at the island from the Cumberland fells above my home. I had seen it on bright summer days floating on the dark sea, and in winter when the snow glistened on its peaks. I had an irresistible urge to explore it; but what was I to find? The books I read told of Viking raiders, smugglers, enchanted glens and fairies; of contented people tending a few sheep beside thatched cottages or catching fish in placid waters. But this was the island of the folklorist. Radio, television and newspapers told a very different story. The Manx fishing industry and its famous kipper trade were declining rapidly, and the boom in package tours to the sun-drenched beaches of Spain and the Mediterranean was seriously damaging the island's tourist industry. Manx people were complaining that their Government had vested the salvation of the island in the hands of a few tax exiles, who, if the wind from the British Treasury suddenly blew cold, might transfer their pots of gold to warmer climes, creating immense economic problems. Jobs were scarce, and it was generally believed that the bubble of post-war prosperity had burst and the island was heading for the doldrums.

'Don't believe everything you read in the papers!' declared a Manx lady I knew who had married a Cumbrian and settled in Whitehaven. 'The world might change, but the Isle of Man doesn't. Go and see for yourself!'

2

An Irate Vet and Dirty Nightcaps

The ship steadily increased speed as the last buoy marking the channel to Heysham harbour was left behind, bouncing like a cork in the seething mass of white foam churned up by the propellers. As if at a signal, hordes of white gulls appeared, following the ship like a winged escort, wheeling and dipping as they squabbled over garbage flung from the galley. A solitary seal stuck his head out of the water hoping a titbit might come his way but, realizing he was no match for the gulls, sank beneath the surface and was gone.

It was a beautiful, warm sunny day and the passengers crowded onto the deck, sprawling across the seats or lining the rail to stare as Blackpool Tower and the Lancashire coast slowly dissolved in a purple haze. The bar was doing a roaring trade, helped along towards record takings by several coachloads of Welshmen on their way to compete in sporting events on the island. Packed into the saloon, they gripped pints of beer in unsteady hands and bellowed chorus after chorus of 'Sospan Fach' and 'Guide me, O Thou great Jehovah', all with that incredible gift for harmonizing which seems to come naturally to the Welsh whether they are standing stiffly in chapel or staggering home after a rugby celebration. Attracted by the singing, more and more people pushed their way into the bar, until they overflowed onto the deck in a mass of sweating bodies and empty beer glasses.

'Where's the gents, boyo?' groaned one of the choir as he crawled past me on hands and knees, eyes glazed, his supporter's scarf trailing behind him.

'It's just a few yards along the deck; keep going!' I replied encouragingly.

But he failed to reach it. To the disgust of an elderly gentleman quietly engrossed in his newspaper and to the horror of a teacher in charge of a party of schoolgirls, he staggered to his feet, clung to the rail and with a loud sigh of relief peed into the sea.

Escaping from yet another rendering of 'Guide me, O Thou great Jehovah' and shouts of 'Wales forever!' from the bar, I went below deck to the dining saloon in search of a meal.

I had finished eating and was sipping my tea when an announcement over the public address system asked me to call at the Chief Steward's office.

'So you're the chap who held us up,' said the Chief Steward with a wide grin. 'The Captain would like to see you. Follow me!' He led the way through a door marked 'Crew Only' and we climbed a series of stairways to the ship's bridge. A tall man in uniform turned as we entered.

'This is Mr Orrell, Captain,' said the Chief Steward. The Captain smiled and held out his hand.

'Hello,' he said, 'I'm Ken Crellin. Welcome aboard. For a while it looked as if we would have to leave without you.'

'I'm really grateful for your help,' I said. 'If I'd missed the sailing, it would have meant cancelling my journey and returning home.'

'Well, you're not in the clear yet,' said the Captain. 'My instructions are that you have got to take the certificate for the ponies to the Government Veterinary Surgeon in Douglas tomorrow morning before you set off on your travels. Whatever you do, don't forget, or there'll be all hell let loose. Meantime, relax and enjoy the trip. You can stay on the bridge if you want; there'll be a mug of tea coming up soon.'

He turned away to speak to a member of the crew, and I settled myself in a seat beside a vast console of dials and switches that whirred and ticked, keeping the huge ship on course for Douglas. The view through the windows was magnificent and, apart from the occasional voice blaring out of the ship-to-shore radio and the clicking instruments, it was remarkably quiet.

Passengers on a ship are not often invited to the bridge, and the carousers in the bar and those snoozing peacefully in the lounges or watching video films would have been impressed by the vigilance of the ship's officers in looking after their safety. Although it was a perfect day, with a calm sea and excellent visibility, the officers regularly scanned the sea through binoculars and stared intently at the radar screen. Everything was checked, then double-checked; position of the ship marked on the chart, log entered up, course adjusted, engine speed increased slightly or reduced, a wary eye kept on a fishing boat or yacht passing close by – all done with hardly a word spoken as the ship sliced through the sea at full speed carrying over 700 passengers and nearly 200 vehicles.

The afternoon passed quickly, and soon the island appeared on the horizon – a dark smudge at first, but as we drew closer, the summit of Snaefell took shape and whitewashed houses stood out against a background of green hills.

Activity on the bridge increased as messages passed between the ship and the Harbourmaster at Douglas, and on deck the crew began to uncoil mooring lines in readiness to heave them ashore. The lighthouse marking the entrance to the harbour came into view, and behind it the town of Douglas, its brightly painted hotels and houses curving in a kaleidoscope of colour around the edge of the bay. With a long blast on the siren, the ship steamed slowly into the harbour, and the Captain, operating the engine controls from the wing of the bridge, skilfully swung it round and manoeuvred it backwards until the steel door of the vehicle hold was positioned neatly on a ramp leading up to the quay. A large sign painted on a wall said, 'Welcome to the Isle of Man.'

I made my way down to the vehicle deck and opened the door of the horsebox. Except for a short trip across Loch Linnhe in Scotland, which almost ended in disaster when Lucy tried to jump over the side of the ferry, the ponies had never been to sea, and I wondered what effect four hours in the hold of a ship would have had on them.

Thor is a very lovable old pony but he is an incurable coward, and almost from the day he was born he has been frightened of loud noises, things that flap in the wind, swishing bicycles and people who run towards him (unless, of course, they are brandishing a bar of chocolate or a bag of sweets). By the expression on his face it was obvious that 'the lonely sea and the sky' were not for him: he stood rigid, like a piece of sculptured black marble, eyes staring and beads of perspiration dripping from his neck.

Lucy, on the other hand, had soon got used to the motion of the ship and had spent the time champing through her pile of hay, and Thor's as well when his hay net swung in her direction. Very different from Thor in temperament and build, she was a courageous little pony and it took a lot to really upset her. She could be infuriatingly independent though, and if she decided she did not want to go into a horsebox or clamber up mountains or cross rivers, nothing on earth would persuade her otherwise. But she had a weakness – she revelled in lots of attention and praise, and both she and Thor loved mints. I gave them a handful to crunch while I drove the horsebox off the ship to the car park in front of the sea terminal building.

When I first started to make preparations for my journey to the Isle of Man, a Manx journalist, Harvey Briggs, wrote about me in one of his articles, and several people on the island telephoned offering help and accommodation. Frank Keig, President of the Isle of Man Light Horse Society, was particularly helpful and he had arranged to meet me off the boat. He introduced himself, and while we chatted he handed over a list of people who were willing to let me camp and graze the ponies each night.

I had planned to start my journey from East Baldwin, near Douglas, and having promised to visit Frank and his family when I reached Kirk Michael, I drove out of Douglas on a perfect evening with the sun streaming through the canopy of trees overhanging the narrow winding roads. A few miles outside the town the road crossed the River Glass into the East Baldwin valley, where I had arranged to spend my first night at Booilshuggel Farm and leave the horsebox and car while I was away on my journey. Philip Caley, the owner, greeted me very warmly and, with Thor and Lucy comfortably bedded down in a barn, I made a meal in the horsebox and crawled wearily into my sleeping-bag.

A loud clanging noise woke me next morning, and when I opened the door I looked straight into the bloodshot eyes of an enormous Charolais bull, scratching his head vigorously and snorting through the steel door of his pen, a few feet from the box.

'He's quite friendly, really,' laughed Philip, appearing out of a feed store holding a bale of hay. 'He just wants to play.' The whole pen shuddered as the bull butted the gate 'playfully', and I retreated to the safety of the barn to see Thor and Lucy.

'Where are you heading for today?' asked Philip, as I set about unravelling the knots in Thor's mane. I told him about the problems at Heysham, and that I had been instructed to report to the Government vet in Douglas.

'Oh, they're very strict about these things,' said Philip, 'but come on down to the house. The vet's name is Davidson, and I know him quite well. I'll phone him and ask what he wants you to do.'

When bureaucrats are being pompous, it can be very irritating, but when they are bureaucrats, Manx Government vets and very angry, it is positively terrifying – and Mr Davidson was all of these. I could hear his voice on the other end of the phone rising higher and higher as Philip attempted to explain how I had arrived on the island with my ponies.

Finally Philip turned and handed me the telephone: 'He wants to speak to you.'

'Hello,' I said, taking care not to hold the instrument too close to my ear.

'Would you mind explaining how you managed to bring two ponies onto the island without the proper authority?' the voice demanded. Full of apologies I launched into my story, but he was out for blood. 'Do you realize you have contravened every rule in the book, and it is a very serious offence? I would be within my rights to impound both animals, and you could be prosecuted. It is my job to ensure that the island is kept free of disease.'

'Look,' I said, trying not to sound angry, but he was making me feel as if I had just arrived from a leper colony, and my hackles were rising. 'I can appreciate your concern, and I am sorry, but it is easily proved that I have only travelled from Cumberland, and I have a certificate proving that the ponies are healthy, so can I post it to you and get on with my journey?'

I had said the wrong thing!

'No, you damn well can't post it to me!' he exploded. 'Leave those animals exactly where they are and bring the certificate to my office this morning.'

'But I'm miles away from Douglas,' I protested, 'and I'll lose a whole day if I have to come in.'

'That's your problem,' he replied. 'You must not leave until I have seen the certificate of health.'

'I could come into Douglas on horseback,' I suggested mischievously. He snorted angrily and put the phone down.

'I think the best thing to do is for me to run you into Douglas in the Landrover,' said Philip when I told him what the vet had said. 'It might help if I took you to the Department of Agriculture myself.'

The town was bursting with holiday-makers, and we searched in vain for a parking space. Eventually Philip neatly manoeuvred the Landrover behind a car on a private parking area at the rear of the Government offices.

'It's the vet's car,' said Philip with a wry smile, 'and we know he won't be leaving his office for a while.'

The office block, although built on the attractive façade of the original government building, was similar to the seats of bureaucracy to be found anywhere in the British Isles. Identical staircases lead to identical rows of doors, which, if left ajar, reveal by a glance at the floor covering, ranging from plain linoleum to wall-to-wall carpet, the status of the occupant in the pecking order. Philip led the way through a maze of corridors to a reception window in the Department of Agriculture, and when a man sitting at a desk saw us he got up and came to greet Philip.

'Hello. How are things at Booilshuggel?'

'Fine, thanks,' replied Philip. 'One or two problems here and there, but nothing to complain about.' He half turned to me: 'This is Mr Orrell. He's brought the papers for his ponies.'

I handed over the certificate and the man examined it carefully to make sure it was in order, then, looking up with a broad smile on his face, he said: 'You've certainly caused quite a stir. We'd better have your full particulars.'

I wrote my name and address on a form, where I'd come from, how long I intended to stay and whether the ponies had been ill recently, and signed it. The man said it was all he needed, apologized for the trouble it had caused me and hoped I would enjoy my stay on the island.

'Thank goodness we saw that friendly chap,' I said to Philip as we made our way outside. 'He was much more helpful than that grumpy old sod Davidson I spoke to on the phone.'

Philip looked at me for a moment, then started laughing. 'That was Mr Davidson we've just been speaking to!' he said.

It was well past mid-day when we got back to the farm, and Philip's wife, Margaret, invited me to stay for lunch. Their young son Jim joined us, and the conversation turned to the weather. It had been a beautiful warm morning, but through the kitchen window we could see dark clouds creeping across the sky from the west.

'The forecast on Manx Radio this morning wasn't too good,' said Philip. 'They were promising rain by late afternoon, and by the look of that sky they won't be far wrong.'

By the time lunch was over it was clear that the weather was going to follow the pattern that had dominated my earlier venture into the Scottish Highlands: the sun faded rapidly, thick cloud advanced across the sky and overflowed onto the tops of the hills, the air became cooler and the cheerful valley was lost in sombre shadows.

Even the ponies sensed the change. Thor, never keen on exercise even in the best of conditions, did his best to shrink his large frame into a dark corner of the barn. Unfortunately for him, the flashing of his greedy teeth pulling at a hay net gave him away. Lucy was sullen and grumpy and refused to co-operate when I buckled on the pack-saddle and harness. It was a sure sign of bad weather. Lucy's moods forecast the weather more accurately than all the barometers, bundles of seaweed, fir cones and satellite photographs put together, and as I loaded the packs onto the saddle she made it very clear she would much prefer to stay in the comfortable barn. Saddlebags carrying cameras, films, chocolate and a large supply of mints were tied firmly behind my old army saddle on Thor, and we were ready to go.

'Where are you planning to stay tonight?' Philip asked as I led the ponies past the house.

'I'm not sure yet,' I replied. 'I want to go over the hill to Laxey, then perhaps up Laxey Glen to camp at the foot of Snaefell.'

'Well, on the map you'll see a place called Llergyrhenny, just below Snaefell on the Sulby road. There's a big shed there owned by a friend of mine who farms at Laxey. I'll phone and ask him to unlock it for you.'

'That's marvellous,' I said. 'The way the weather's turning, I might be glad of it. Goodbye, and thanks for your help.'

'Enjoy yourself!' he called back, and with a wave he climbed onto a tractor and roared off to join Jim in one of the fields.

The sun popped through with an apologetic beam of encouragement, but it was quickly overpowered by snarling clouds. I was grateful for the effort though, and was in good spirits as I left the farmyard and turned Thor towards the head of the valley, tapping my heels against his side to signal that I would appreciate at least a fast walk. There was no response: he placed one leg in front of the other with the minimum effort required to keep moving in a forward direction, and no more. Still in a foul mood, Lucy plodded grumpily behind him.

'What a miserable pair you are,' I cried. 'We're supposed to be enjoying ourselves. Get a move on!'

The pace remained the same. In retaliation I unwrapped a mint and crunched it noisily. Two pairs of ears shot up in expectation.

'Too late,' I jeered. 'The motto for today is "No movement – no mints".'

The snail's pace did at least give me time to admire the scenery, and it was a delight to meander gently along the narrow road flanked by unspoilt hedgerows ablaze with wild flowers. I had read a lot about the Isle of Man, and now, visiting it for the first time, I was very impressed. When the glaciers sculpted the island landscape, it was done less brutally than in other mountainous regions, and Nature's artistry created picturesque glens and fertile plains strewn haphazardly around a hotch-potch of rolling hills.

Thor's back was a good vantage-point, and I could see East Baldwin curving in an attractive blend of fertile fields and barren hillsides between the steep slopes of Slieau Ree on one side, and on the other a long spur rising steadily to the summits of Carraghan and Beinn-y-Phott at the valley head. Not even the threat of approaching bad weather spoiled the excitement of being on the move again with Thor and Lucy, and I burst into song as we moved slowly towards the hills.

Rounding a bend in the road, Thor jerked to a halt and very nearly pitched me out of the saddle. At first I thought it was his way of complaining about my singing but, looking ahead, I could see that the road was partially blocked by a farm trailer which had lost a wheel. Three men leaning on the trailer watched curiously as we approached.

'Hey, do you happen to be carrying a spare wheel on the packhorse?' one of them joked, as I slid off Thor to lead him past the obstruction. I laughed, and said the best I could do was a set of horseshoes, but I would ride back down the valley and get help for them if they needed it.

'Thanks for the offer,' the man said, 'but the wheel bearing has seized up and there's a mechanic coming from Douglas to fix it.'

His two mates were looking closely at Lucy and the pack-saddle.

'By heavens,' said one, 'I've never seen anything like this. You can just imagine what it must have been like on the island in the old days. Everything would have been carried on ponies. I bet it was a grand sight!'

'The way the price of petrol's going you might be seeing it again sooner than you think,' grumbled the other, who was older and obviously considered himself more knowledgeable in the ways of the world. 'I heard tell there's a farmer near Port St Mary gone and bought a Clydesdale to work the farm.'

His mate snorted contemptuously. 'Huh! The farmers are the last ones as'll starve to death. Likely they'll be griping about the price of diesel so they can buy a bloody horse.'

'Look, I'm not having that,' the older man said heatedly. 'If it wasn't for farmers on the island, your missus would be paying twice as much for food; and what about milk? Every drop would have to come over by boat.'

His mate cleared his throat and spat into the hedgerow. 'I've never heard so much bull! You're only saying it because your brother's a farmer.'

It was developing into a full-scale row, but fortunately the arrival of the mechanic in his van diverted their attention to the problem of the trailer. The mechanic was a small, energetic man who leapt out of his van in a flurry of toolboxes and hydraulic jacks. He blinked when he saw the ponies.

'Hell's bells,' he said laughingly, 'nobody mentioned these on the 'phone. Have I been called out to fix a trailer or shoe horses?' He looked at the ponies and then at me. 'You must be the chap I read about in the paper, who's travelling round the island on horseback.'

I smiled and nodded.

'Well, you'd better take a photograph of us then,' he continued, 'for we're a dying breed; real Manx we are, and there aren't many of us left.'

'Quite right, that!' said one of the others. 'Take our photo; they might hang it in the Manx Museum one day.'

They lined up against the trailer, and I dutifully snapped a few pictures of them.

The wind was rising, and thick banks of cloud were beginning to creep threateningly down Beinn-y-Phott at the head of the valley as I climbed into the saddle, anxious to cross the hills to Laxey before the weather broke.

'You'd better get a move on,' warned one of the men. 'There's a saying on the island that when Mona's mountains wear dirty nightcaps in the morning, rain will wash 'em clean before night.'

'Thanks for the advice,' I called, as I urged Thor along the road, but my words were lost in the sound of hammering as the mechanic started on the wheelbearing. One of the men had a sudden flush of inspiration and ran after us.

'Can I give the ponies a bite to eat?' he said. 'I've got a spare sandwich.' Before I could protest, ever-hungry Lucy had snatched it out of his hand and devoured it in one gulp. He patted her neck approvingly. 'You enjoyed that, didn't you, girl? It was a nice piece of garlic sausage.'

When the man was out of earshot, I scolded Lucy for being so greedy. 'You never know what's in imported sausage,' I said. 'For all you know, you might have been eating one of your relatives!' She looked at me with such a pained expression in her brown eyes that I was stricken with conscience.

To confirm that Manx weather portents are not just fairy stories, the clouds flung a few drops of rain at the back of my neck while I did my best to convey to Thor that there was a certain amount of urgency in the situation, but as usual he took not the slightest bit of notice.

After a mile or so, the surfaced road gave out, and the map showed a path striking diagonally up the open hillside to the Douglas to Ramsey mountain road, before descending again to Glen Roy and Laxey. At first a well-defined lane climbed between dilapidated dry-stone walls, but high on the hillside it petered out, and a twisted iron gate marked the boundary of what had once been several small farmsteads, whose scattered ruins lay in the grass – a silent epitaph to the harshness of life in the hills a century or more ago. Despite the threatening cloud and the occasional spot of rain, it was remarkably warm, and I lay in the heather enjoying the view.

The Manx landscape is often compared with the hills of mid-Wales, Ireland, south Scotland or parts of Yorkshire and Derbyshire, but to me it is unique. It has a certain mystical charm and, while lacking the grandeur of towering crags and sharp peaks, is always varied and exciting. The East Baldwin landscape is an artist's paradise but, not being gifted in that direction, I had to content myself with capturing it through the lens of a camera. It was a large droplet of rain landing on the camera lens and distorting the picture in the viewfinder that warned me of approaching bad weather and, gathering the ponies, I continued on up the hill.

There was no sign of a path above the gate, but the ground was firm, and Thor had no difficulty in traversing the steep heather. The angle soon eased, and a short ride across an expanse of dry bog brought us to the main road at Windy Corner. I was relieved to find a gate in the fence, but it took over an hour to unravel yards of rusty chain, lead the ponies through, then wind it all back again. The track to Glen Roy was there all right, but the entrance was barred by a cattle grid and there was no way through for animals. I searched up and down, but there was no way onto the track except by the cattle grid.

'Fancy building a cattle grid and not putting a gate by it!' I complained aloud to the ponies. 'What a damned stupid thing to do.'

It started to drizzle, and a cool wind flung the moisture in my face as I struggled into my waterproof suit and sheltered behind Thor, searching the map for another route to Ramsey. The only alternative involved using the main road, and I wanted to avoid that at all costs. Going back to the cattle grid again, I considered jumping the ponies over it, but a slip would have been disastrous. Then I hit on an idea. Close by the cattle grid was an old wall, which had long since outlived its purpose and been replaced by a wire fence. Large, flat stones from the wall were scattered around and, gathering them up, I placed them in rows over the grid. It was a laborious, time-consuming task, and a mixture of rain and sweat ran down my face, but eventually the bars of the grid were safely covered and the ponies crossed without a murmur. Feeling very pleased with myself, I was busily returning the stones to the wall when a car, bulging with barking dogs and driven by a woman, turned off the main road and stopped abruptly in front of the grid.

'I say, what do you think you are doing?' she demanded, winding the car window down. Immediately the dogs

barked louder and leapt for the opening in a snarling
tangle of terriers, spaniels, bulldogs and a flat-faced
Pekinese, about to yap its last under the weight of a huge,
slobbering Great Dane. The woman beat them back,
shouting, 'Down, Towser, you oaf. Simba, how dare you?
Pippa, you are being beastly. Sit down this instant! Oh, my
poor Kwang Fu! Are you all right, my precious?' until they
retreated in a cowering heap onto the back seat of the car.
Then she turned her attention to me again. 'Well, what are
you doing to the cattle grid?'

'I'm not doing anything to it,' I said. 'I'm simply using a
few stones to get my ponies across, because there isn't a
gate to go through.'

'You have absolutely no right to spread stones over the
cattle grid,' she shrilled. 'Why should we provide gates for
the likes of you? What are you, anyway, a hobo?'

I gritted my teeth. 'No, madam, I am not a hobo,' I said
slowly. 'Actually, I am a writer, but I don't suppose there's
a great deal of difference.'

Her attitude immediately changed. 'A writer,' she
cooed, as if she were sure I was about to confess modestly
that I was Hammond Innes or Jeffrey Archer. 'I say, do
tell me your name!'

When I told her, she could hardly conceal her
disappointment. 'Can't say I've heard of you,' she
sniffed, 'but then my husband and I seldom read anything
unless it is by one of the great authors.'

I had heard enough. Heaving the last of the stones off
the cattle grid, I climbed into the saddle.

'If you're the owner of the land, perhaps you won't
mind if I use the track to get to Glen Roy,' I said brusquely.

'Oh, I'm not the owner,' she replied. 'We have a house in
the north of the island. We were farming in Africa you
know, but the naughty tax man wanted too much when we
returned to London, so my husband decided to come
here. I told him he was mad, but the poor darling wouldn't
listen.' She lowered her voice: 'Actually, to be honest,' she
confessed, 'we both absolutely loathe the place. The Manx
people are frightfully stupid, and you just wouldn't believe
how insolent they can be. I really don't know why we stay,

but my husband says they depend on us.' The dogs started barking again and she looked at her watch. 'Oh, the poor dears!' she exclaimed. 'It's way past their lunchtime. I must be off.' With a loud grinding of gears, the car lurched backwards onto the main road, and she drove away.

'There goes one of the reasons why the British Empire fell apart at the seams,' I confided to Thor and Lucy, as we clattered down the stony track towards Glen Roy.

Early in the nineteenth century, when most London newspapers were agog with the latest escapades of Napoleon Bonaparte, an advertisement appeared which brought temporary relief from the activities of the ambitious Frenchman by focusing attention on a little-known island in the Irish Sea.

> To those possessed of limited means – to half-pay officers, retired tradesmen of moderate fortune and small amenities – the following information is addressed. The situation pointed out offers a retirement within the pale of the British dominions, within easy reach of friends, in a healthful climate; of a comparatively cheap rate of living. The Isle of Man is situated about the middle of the Irish Channel – as a sea-bathing place, Douglas can scarcely be surpassed; whether the salubrity of the climate, or the purity of the water, be considered; and it possesses excellent accommodation both for warm and cold bathing. The Isle of Man is totally free from taxes, except a rate upon dogs, public houses, and a very small rate upon dwelling houses in the towns; the sums thus raised being applied to the repairing of the highways ...

A large number of army officers who had retired on half pay came to take advantage of the low cost of living, but keeping up appearances and moving in the right circles were a drain on their meagre resources, and they often found that the glowing accounts of the Utopia in the Irish Sea were founded more on rumour than reality.

In his *Memoirs and Confessions* published around 1815,

Captain Thomas Ashe, a native of Dublin, wrote: 'Possessing now my half pay, clear of all embarrassment, and the accumulated pay of five years, or one hundred and fifty pounds in hand, I formed the resolution of retiring to some cheap place, and of living independent of the world, on my own contracted means. I chose the Isle of Man; but so little did the project succeed, that I spent nearly all my ready money, and was considerably in debt in the course of two years …'

With growth in tourism at the turn of the century the island's economy was less dependent on the money retired people brought with them, but as the British Empire steadily declined and the tea-planters, farmers, colonial officers, oil-company employees and ex-army officers returned for one reason or another to Britain, they found the attentions of the tax man not to their liking and, hastily seeking a more agreeable resting place, were attracted by the Isle of Man. Business financiers and show-business personalities realized that, as air communication between the island and London improved, they would be in easy commuting distance of their offices and theatres, and arrived on house-hunting jaunts.

Soon the postbags of London stockbrokers bulged with changes of address as Pickford's removal vans, crammed with African spears, elephants carved in ivory, Indian carpets, showbiz nostalgia and memorabilia from all corners of the globe, thundered north to catch the Isle of Man steamers. The tax exiles injected a new wealth into the island, and the Manx people benefited from it. But there were problems.

In 1794, David Robertson, a visitor to the island, wrote in his book *A Tour Through the Isle of Man*: 'The harmony … is sometimes marred by mutual prejudices. In many of the natives, notwithstanding a show of politeness and hospitality, there is a secret aversion to strangers: and in several of the English an unreasonable contempt of the Manx.'

On my travels round the island nearly 200 years later I was to discover that there had been little change.

3

Laxey Wheel and Llergyrhenny

The storm which had been threatening all morning arrived with a vengeance as the ponies picked their way down the stony path towards Glen Roy, and wave after wave of torrential rain swept in from the sea, driven by a fierce wind. There was not a scrap of shelter to be found on the open hillside, and poor Lucy suffered a tremendous buffeting as the wind tore at the packs and tried its best to knock her over. Thor showed every sign of returning rapidly to Philip Caley's barn but, crouching low over his neck to escape the blasts, I could vaguely make out the way ahead and, shouting what I hoped were words of encouragement in his ear, I kept him moving forward.

We had staggered along for a mile or so when mercifully the track started down to a gate, and behind it high banks and hedgerows sheltered us from the storm. Freed from the grip of the wind, the rain now descended vertically in monsoon proportions, but at least I could sit upright in the saddle without having to cling onto Thor's mane like Tam o'Shanter fleeing from the Devil. The lane joined a narrow, surfaced road which wound round to a cluster of attractive cottages at the head of Glen Roy before climbing steeply up again to level out at the edge of a forest plantation overlooking Laxey Bay. At least, the map showed that it overlooked Laxey Bay, but apart from odd glimpses of grey landscape far below when the rain occasionally eased from torrential to vigorously wet, visibility was never more than a few hundred yards.

Attracted by a patch of grass among the trees, Lucy wandered into the wood while I was busy attending to

Thor's girth and, taking the hint, I let them have a break while I sheltered from the rain behind a wall. To prevent Thor straying, I tethered him to a tree on a long rope, and had just settled myself against the wall when he started to whinny. I looked up to find he had grazed in a circle and had wound the rope round so tightly that his nose was pressed against the tree trunk. It took a good five minutes to unwind him, and I had hardly returned to the shelter of the wall when the pathetic whinnying started again.

'The next time you bang your silly nose on the tree,' I said irritably as I untangled the rope, 'all you have to do is eat in an anti-clockwise direction and you'll free yourself.' He was whinnying again before I had even reached the wall. I slowly peeled an orange and ignored him.

The wind pounced on us again when we left the shelter of the wood, and the ride down the long hill to Laxey will be remembered only for the number of times Lucy was bowled over by the blasts or Thor lost his footing on the wet tarmac as the salt-laden squalls roared in from the sea. It was an immense relief to reach the houses on the edge of the village, and the ponies surged ahead with renewed energy, sending up clouds of spray as they splashed through pools of water lying in the road.

Not even the most ardent lovers of the Isle of Man could argue that Laxey is the prettiest village on the island, and its deserted streets, flanked by rows of cottages built during the nineteenth-century mining boom, were grim and depressing in the rain; but at least it was a change from the windswept hills, and a point in its favour was that it had a shelter. It was really intended for passengers waiting for the Snaefell mountain railway, but since it was unoccupied I hoped the owners would not mind Thor and Lucy using it as a temporary stable while I re-arranged the packs and saddle blankets and brewed a mug of coffee on my paraffin stove. The hot drink warmed me through and, snug inside the shelter, I was in no hurry to face the downpour again, though when the driver of a passing car stopped his vehicle, reversed and glared at us before driving off at high speed, I feared he was going for the police.

Pulling the two reluctant ponies after me, I crossed the railway line and joined the road to Laxey Glen and the great waterwheel. There is hardly a Manx Tourist Board brochure to be found that does not include at least one photograph of Laxey Wheel, and it is a great tourist attraction. Seen from a distance it looks like a brightly coloured fairground wheel, and as I approached, it was the one spark of cheerfulness in an otherwise dismal background of waterlogged trees and grey swirling mist. It was hardly the weather for sightseeing, but I could not miss the opportunity to visit the wheel.

Leaving Thor and Lucy chewing an apple apiece in the shelter of a tall hedge, I followed a narrow path to a kiosk, bought a ticket and two little books about the history of the wheel, and crossed a footbridge to pay my respects to Lady Isabella.

When they were in full production, the mines at Laxey produced more zinc ore than all the mines in the British Isles put together, and the lead ore was particularly rich in silver. Before the mines could operate, there were enormous technical problems to overcome, not least how to remove 250 gallons of floodwater per minute from a depth of 1,800 feet. In other areas of Britain it would have been easily overcome by using steam-driven pumps but, the island having no coal resources, it would have meant bringing every piece in by sea. It was Robert Casement, the mining company's engineer, who solved it. His idea for a pump powered by a waterwheel raised a few eyebrows, but he got his way and set about building one of the largest waterwheels in the world, a monument to his own inventive genius. Not only was the wheel gigantic, over seventy-two feet in diameter by six feet wide, it could not be built directly over the mine shaft and was sited 200 yards away, with an ingenious system of rods operating the water pump. The wheel was officially opened on Wednesday, 27 September, 1854.

'The day being beautifully fine, between 3,000 and 4,000 persons arrived from all parts of the island ... to witness so great an achievement for our little isle as the completion of the largest wheel in Europe ... Simultaneously with the first motion of the wheel the ceremony of christening was performed by Mrs Dumbell, lady of Geo. W. Dumbell Esq., who gracefully threw the bottle, ornamented with lace and filled with champagne, and named the wheel "Lady Isabella" in honour of the Governor's lady.'

One of the books I bought at the kiosk boasted that, 'The climb up the ninety-six steps to the platform of the tower is well worth the effort for the sake of the glorious views over the Glen and out to sea.' Since it was pouring with rain and I could barely see the top of the tower from the ground, I found difficulty in sharing the writer's enthusiasm; and in any case the other book was more accurate, claiming only ninety-five steps to the top, and water flowing under your feet when you reached it. The tower was part of the structure supporting the wheel, and at first I could not understand why the steps were attached to the outside of the tower rather than inside it. The official guide-book revealed all. With a touch of Casement genius, the water driving the wheel was piped up the centre of the tower. Gripping the handrail firmly, I climbed the slippery steps to the platform and looked down on its massive axle, giving an impression of immense power.

After the Laxey mines closed in 1929, the wheel was abandoned, and had it not been for Mr Edwin Kneale, a local builder, it would have crumbled into obscurity. Appreciating its value as a tourist attraction, the Manx Government eventually acquired it from Mr Kneale, and after extensive restoration it was re-opened in 1970. As I stared down from the top of the tower, I could not help thinking that it was a shame the wheel could not be put to some practical use, such as generating electricity, rather than towering above the landscape like a giant eunuch whose once productive parts had been reduced to the level of a tourist spectacle.

Thor and Lucy were dozing peacefully under the hedge when I returned from my visit to the wheel, and were not at all happy about moving on again. Even when bribed with mints they plodded along so agonizingly slowly I was convinced that, had it not been for a strong wind from behind us, they would have walked backwards!

'Thor, will you please get a move on?' I pleaded, drumming my heels into his hairy sides. 'We've only a short distance to go, then you can rest and eat for hours.'

I was telling lies really. Snaefell, where I had planned to

camp, was still some distance away, but I would have told him anything to stir him into action. The plea fell on deaf ears, and he even had the cheek to stop and nibble at a patch of grass. I whacked his rump with Lucy's lead rope and he trundled forward, almost breaking into a run.

At the hamlet of Agneash, far above the shelter of Laxey village, the wind was blowing a gale and combined with the heavy rain it was very uncomfortable. I considered looking for a place to camp, but I reasoned that the wind was unlikely to change direction and would be on our backs all the way up to Snaefell, and if it got worse I was sure I could find shelter in some old mine workings marked on the map at the head of Laxey Glen. Decision made, I zipped my waterproof jacket up to my neck, tightened the hood cords, checked the packs and girth straps, and with the wind doing its best to blow us over Snaefell we set off. The track was wide and had a good surface, and with the ponies going strongly I had nothing to do but occasionally glance back to see that all was well with Lucy. Draping Thor's reins over the saddle I pulled my hands inside my sleeves, and basked in the warmth and security of my waterproof suit.

The view between Thor's ears was a narrow, moving picture of low cloud, saturated hillside and swollen streams foaming across the track. Sometimes a derelict building, an abandoned wall or a few sheep crouching miserably behind a boulder would loom onto the screen, then fade out of the side like a 3D movie. But it was no silent movie – the dull thud of the ponies' hooves sounding above the roar of the wind like amplified heartbeats would easily have earned it a 'horror' category.

I was snapped out of my daydream by Lucy's lead rope being jerked off my saddle, and I turned to find the pack-saddle leaning at an angle and Lucy looking very upset, as if she was afraid I might blame her for it.

'It's not your fault,' I said, slipping her a piece of chocolate when Thor was looking the other way. 'The rain has made everything very loose. You're doing fine. Not far to go now.'

She blinked the rain out of her eyes and patiently munched the chocolate while I unbuckled the girth strap and heaved the saddle upright.

With the strong wind pushing us along, it took a little over an hour to cover the two miles to the abandoned Snaefell mine, and though only the walls of the buildings remained, they were high enough to protect us from the wind. There was not a solitary blade of grass for the ponies to eat, and I felt rather guilty as I pumped the paraffin stove into life to heat a pan of soup.

Abandoned buildings look ghostly at the best of times, but shrouded in mist and dripping with water they feel positively eerie. Huddled in a corner with my mug of soup, I was conscious of every sound. Water cascading down a subterranean cavern vibrated the ground beneath my feet, and when the wind moaned around the slag heaps and dislodged boulders, they crashed down into a deep ravine between the buildings as if the whole hillside was disintegrating. Having read about the Snaefell mine disaster, I had the uneasy feeling that the spirits of the dead miners were watching from every doorway and dark corner.

Close to where I was sitting, the miners turned up for work one Monday morning in May 1897, laughing and joking after the walk from their homes in Laxey. Checking that they had their candles and lunch boxes, the men gathered at the top of the shaft and one by one descended the ladder to reach the workface hundreds of feet below. Writers of books about the Isle of Man have different versions of what happened after the men went down the shaft, but according to the official Home Office report twenty men died that day, due to poisonous gas caused by a fire smouldering in the mine timbers nearly 800 feet down.

The thought of it made me shiver and, hurriedly packing the stove, I led the ponies outside and away from the mine. The wind was still blowing and the mist was as thick as ever, but the map showed that the head of the glen was only a short distance from the main road below Snaefell. The contours indicated a fairly steep slope, but I calculated that, by striking diagonally up it, we would come to the fence bordering the road and perhaps find a gate.

For a while I followed a grassy path which seemed to be heading in the right direction, but it soon disappeared, and within minutes we were floundering in a bog and I realized I had absolutely no idea where I was. Accustomed to travelling in more rugged country, I had underestimated the little hills of the Isle of Man and had not bothered to work out a compass bearing. Caught in the teeth of a gale, and with visibility down to a few yards, there were no landmarks to take a bearing, and I was lost.

I knew that in the mist somewhere above me was the main road, and to reach it I would now have to strike directly up the hill. It was too steep to ride, and to ease the strain on Lucy I tied one of the packs to Thor's saddle. Blinded by the rain and buffeted by the wind, the three of us were gasping for breath before we had gone more than a few hundred yards, and to make matters worse, the hill was scarred with deep gullies, and long detours had to be made to avoid them. The sound of a lorry passing close by in the mist was music to my ears, for I knew we had almost reached the road, and sure enough a few more floundering steps brought us to the fence. Close by was a fast-flowing stream pouring down a deep gully and, identifying it on the map, I was relieved to discover we were only about a quarter of a mile from the Bungalow station where the Snaefell Mountain Railway crossed the road. The only disadvantage was that in following the fence we were broadside on to the wind and rain, and for most of the way the ponies walked along with one eye closed.

I hoped to find a shelter similar to the one in Laxey, but the Bungalow station turned out to be no more than a stopping place for the train, so I had to make do with resting Thor and Lucy behind the wall of an evil-smelling public toilet. It was a disgustingly filthy place, littered with broken glass, empty beer cans, used toilet paper and cigarette packets, and I was amazed that on an island sensitive about its tourist image the authorities could tolerate such an eyesore. The smell was so foul it made me feel sick and, preferring the freshness of the rain, I pulled the protesting ponies back onto the road and set off for the shed Philip Caley had arranged for me to use at

Llergyrhenny. Sensing we were on our last lap, the wind gods mustered up all their forces to give us a lively finish to the day. We were absolutely blasted along the road in a fiendish hailstorm that had the ponies leaping with pain.

At first sight Llergyrhenny looked like a farmhouse surrounded by fields but, when I left the main road and followed a track leading to it, I saw that what looked like a house was in fact a large shed alongside a complex of sheep pens. The farmer had very kindly removed the padlocks for me, and I quickly unloaded the packs and saddles and dumped them in a heap inside the shed.

'You've done well today,' I said to Thor and Lucy, patting their necks. 'Get your noses into that grass; you'll be out of the wind by the side of the shed.' I started to close the door but they stood motionless, staring at me with sad expressions on their faces. 'Well, go on then,' I said. 'What are you waiting for? I want to close the door.' Lucy edged a bit closer. Then it dawned on me: 'Surely you don't want to ...' But Lucy did not give me a chance to finish – she was half way through the door. There was no point in arguing! 'Oh, all right then,' I sighed, flinging the door wide open. 'Come on in.'

They were saturated and, finding a ragged towel hanging on a nail, I rubbed them down and draped saddle blankets over their backs to keep them warm. Even with the ponies in the shed, there was still plenty of room, and though it reeked of sheep dip and horse sweat, compared to a tent it was luxury. There was a table and several chairs, and with the harness and my waterproofs festooned from convenient nails in the wall I set about assembling the paraffin stove. I was so hungry the pan of potatoes and corned beef seemed to take ages to cook, but it was worth waiting for. Thor and Lucy looked enviously on as I devoured every scrap and washed it down with a mug of strong coffee.

It was well into the evening by the time the meal was over, and I crawled thankfully into my sleeping-bag and lay listening to the gale raging outside. As each rain squall passed over, it hammered on the corrugated iron roof of the shed like a thousand pneumatic road-drills and shook the building to its foundations. I lit a candle and wrote up the day's events in my diary.

What had pleased me most was that my new waterproof suit had not let a solitary drop of water through, nor was there any sign of condensation inside. The clothes I had worn underneath were completely dry and I was able to sleep in them. Over the years I have tried many different makes of waterproof clothing, and if there is a cloth of the proofed nylon type which keeps water out and at the same time does not suffer from condensation problems, I have yet to find it. I have worn nylon suits and the fisherman's oilskin variety, believing that a little sweat was preferable to a lot of wet, but while they are all right for a day out, wearing them on a long camping trip is a different matter. Occasionally a revolutionary material is launched in a blaze of publicity, but the only way in which it differs from those already on the market is that it is usually considerably more expensive. My new waterproof suit of oiled 'thornproof' material had been made by a well-known firm in South Shields and, though not as light as nylon, it was well worth the extra weight to keep warm and dry.

I dowsed the candle and pulled the sleeping-bag over my head to escape from the noise of the wind and rain, but I could not sleep. During the lulls in the storm, when all was quiet for a few minutes, the ponies stamped on the concrete floor as they shifted their feet.

Almost exhausted by being kept awake, I was just dozing off when I heard a peculiar flapping noise by the door, followed by a few croaks, then the most hideous screech. My blood froze, and I lay rigid, hardly daring to breathe. There was more flapping, then another blood-curdling screech. Grabbing my torch, I snapped it on – and there, perched on one of the chairs, was a large jackdaw staring at me with glowing eyes like Old Nick himself. With another hideous screech he flew into a corner of the shed and disappeared behind a heap of boxes, where he had obviously taken up residence with Mrs Jackdaw. She had produced a brood of little jackdaws, and whether they were just welcoming Dad home or Mrs Jackdaw was giving him hell for being out late, I never did discover, but they set up the most awful din.

The discordant symphony of jackdaws screeching, ponies stamping their feet, and rain drumming on the iron roof put paid to any chance of sleep and, lighting a candle, I browsed through a copy of *Guide to Yoga Meditation* I had found lying on a chair. It could have been the influence of the book or simply that I was completely whacked, but when I woke up the candle had burned to a blob of grease.

It was daylight, and there was not so much as a whisper of wind or a drop of rain to be heard. Looking at my watch, I saw it was six o'clock and, pulling on my boots, I dashed outside to check the weather. It had stopped raining, but thick fog hung everywhere and visibility was down to a few yards. The ponies had eaten nothing all night except for an apple and a few biscuits, and they needed no persuading to leave the shed. Lucy bounded through the door and disappeared into the fog. Thor could not find her and stood outside the door whinnying until he realized he was standing on food and began tearing at the grass. I returned to the warmth of the sleeping-bag and fell instantly asleep.

The dense fog persisted all morning and when I woke I passed the time cleaning the saddles and bridle and coating them with dubbin. Mr and Mrs Jackdaw had several heated disputes, then called a truce and departed in a flurry of smelly feathers to take the little jackdaws on an outing. I had a peep behind the boxes when they had gone, and discovered that the family home was a foul-smelling mound of twigs and droppings about a foot high.

At two o'clock in the afternoon the fog was still as thick as porridge, and I abandoned any hope of leaving that day. With a mug of coffee at my elbow, I curled up in my sleeping-bag and read a bloody account of how the Vikings conquered the island.

Viking history is like Scottish clan history, with lots of heads being chopped off, daggers driven through hearts, and the usual mixture of intrigue and treachery.

It was round about AD 800 that the Isle of Man's 'green hills by the sea' first attracted the Viking marauders, and they enjoyed their stay so much that they returned regularly – too regularly as far as the Manxmen were concerned, for the souvenirs they took away with them were the contents of their houses, their farm animals and their wives and children. The Vikings plundered the island and terrorized the people to such a degree that there was one occasion when, having leapt ashore hell-bent on snaffling another boatload of Manx ladies and hand-knitted sweaters, they found there was not a soul on the whole of the island. The entire population had fled to Scotland. In the course of time the Vikings came to appreciate that the island was a rather nice place to live, and settled in large numbers under their own King of Man.

The origins of the Manx kingdom are explained in great detail in the many learned books on the subject, though some of the best stories would be dismissed by historians as being pure folklore. One lengthy legend tells how a long line of Manx kings came to be descended from Olav Godredson, because a cook fell asleep and the castle he was supposed to be guarding burned down ...

It seems that a Viking nobleman called Kitter had such a passion for hunting that he killed most of the wild animals on the island, and the people, fearing he might start using their cattle for target practice, enlisted the help of Ada, the island witch. One day Kitter left to hunt deer on the Calf of Man, leaving Eaoch, his cook, guarding the castle. Ada seized her chance, and while Eaoch was asleep she caused a pot of fat to boil over onto the kitchen fire and set the castle ablaze. Seeing flames pouring from his castle, Kitter leapt into his boat, but before he reached Man the craft struck a rock and all on board were lost.

Poor Eaoch was not only blamed for the loss of the castle but Olav Godredson, the King, accused him of being in league with witches and sentenced him to death. It was the custom of the Vikings for a criminal to be allowed to choose how he should die, and Eaoch, having worked out a crafty ruse by which he no doubt hoped he would be released to continue his gastronomic career, said: 'I wish my head to be laid across one of Your Majesty's legs, and there cut off by Your Majesty's sword Macabuin, which was made by Loan Maclibhuin, the dark smith of Drontheim.'

The sword was said to be so sharp it could slice through granite, and understandably the King's advisers urged him not to go through with it and simply perforate Eaoch with a dagger. Not wanting to be thought a coward, Olav ordered the execution to go ahead according to Eaoch's wishes, but on the quiet he warned Ada the witch to pull all her sorceress's stops out to ensure he came to no harm. Ada gathered toads' skins, twigs of the rowan tree and adder's eggs, 'each to the number of nine times nine' – no one has explained where, on an island where snakes had been driven away by the holy St Patrick, Ada managed to gather adders' eggs – and placed them between Olav's leg and Eaoch's head. Though the sword was lowered gently onto the neck of the unfortunate cook, its weight severed the head off, but it could not cut through Ada's magical barrier, and the King's leg was saved.

The story might have ended there were it not for Loan, the blacksmith who had made the sword, taking umbrage at what he considered an insult to his skill as a swordmaker. He sent his hammerman, Hiallus, who had lost a leg while helping to make the great sword, to challenge the King to a race from the Isle of Man to the blacksmith's shop at Drontheim, in Norway. Olav could not ignore the challenge and immediately set off, boasting he would soon leave Hiallus far behind. But the hammerman was tougher than he realised, and it was only with a last-minute burst of speed that Olav managed to pip him to the post and run into the smithy. Loan the blacksmith was furious that Hiallus had lost the race, and was even more upset when Olav picked up a large hammer and with a whoop of victory split the anvil in half.

Emergaid, the blacksmith's daughter, on the other hand, was so impressed by this manly display that she fell deeply in love with Olav and warned him that the reason her father had lured him to Drontheim was because it had been prophesied that a new sword he was making would be tempered with royal blood for the revenge of Eaoch's death by the sword Macabuin.

'Is not your father the seventh son of old Windy Cap, King of Norway?'

'He is,' said Emergaid.

'Then,' said Olav, 'the prophecy must be fulfilled!' and, lifting the sword from the forge, he pushed the white-hot steel through Loan as he walked through the door.

With that comforting way legends have of ending happily, Emergaid quickly forgave Olav for disposing of her father and returned to the Isle of Man as his queen. From her were descended all succeeding Kings of Man down to Magnus, who died in 1265. The following year the long and turbulent rule of the Vikings ended when the King of Norway sold the Hebrides and the Isle of Man to the King of Scotland.

It was late in the afternoon before I finished the book about the Vikings, and still the fog showed no sign of lifting. I went outside to share an apple with the ponies, but I lost sight of the shed after walking only a few paces and had to throw stones ahead of me in order to find it again.

Dinner that evening was something of a gastronomic adventure. An outdoor equipment supplier had given me a number of packets of dried food to try out and, with names like 'Chop Suey with Chicken' and 'Rice and Shrimp', they sounded very appetizing. Most dehydrated camping foods have to be simmered twenty minutes or so, but although this new variety required only hot water and a wait of five minutes, the flavours were rather artificial, and whoever thought of the idea forgot that hot water left for five minutes cools to lukewarm.

The jackdaw family arrived back just before dark, and for mother it had obviously been a harrowing day. She cursed and scolded until Father Jackdaw could stand it no longer and flew off to visit his pals. The ranting and raving continued and made such a noise that I shouted: 'For goodness sake, shut up!' and hurled an empty sheep-dip tin at the nest. She poked her head over the boxes and glared at me. I had a feeling that she had never been spoken to like that before. But it had the right effect. I slept undisturbed.

4

Wheneyes and the King of Cars

When I woke the next morning, it was almost nine-thirty, and to my delight bright sunlight was streaming through the windows. Throwing the sleeping-bag off, I rushed outside and could hardly believe my eyes. There was not a cloud in the sky, and in every direction the green hills stood out breathtakingly clear, decorated with thin wisps of mist as the sun mopped up the last drops of moisture. In the field by the shed the ponies were in their favourite positions: Lucy nose down tearing at the grass, Thor stretched out asleep, his great belly rising and falling and shuddering gently like a working model of an earthquake.

'Hey!' I shouted. 'Wake up!' Lucy glanced round to see who was disturbing the peace, then carried on eating. 'Thor, wakey wakey!' I shouted again. His ears twitched and he looked at me balefully with one eye. 'Time to go,' I called cheerfully. He flopped back into the grass and ignored me. I unwrapped a mint and rustled the paper. His ears twitched again and he lumbered to his feet. Lucy sidled over cautiously but accepted a mint while I put her head collar on.

After a quick breakfast I spread the map out on the warm grass to plan my route. To celebrate the thousandth year of Tynwald, the Manx Parliament, a long-distance footpath had been established based on the 'Regia Via', the Royal Way, a very ancient route recorded in the chronicle of the monks of Rushen Abbey towards the end of the fourteenth century. The route, appropriately enough

44

called the Millennium Way, runs the length of the island
from Ramsey in the north to Castletown on the southern
tip, and is about twenty-eight miles long. Although
essentially a footpath, I had been assured that much of it
was passable on horseback, and though I did not want to
stay on it for its entire length, it popped up in many of the
areas I wanted to visit. I had not worked out a particular
route to follow, but I was keen to visit the Point of Ayre
lighthouse on the northernmost point of the island, and
since a section of the Millennium Way passed close to
Llergyrhenny and crossed the hills to Ramsey, it seemed
an ideal way to go.

Leaving the jackdaws a present of a few crumbs of cake,
I fastened the shed door and, with the ponies striding out,
left Llergyrhenny behind and joined the Millennium Way.

For the first half mile the old route was easy to follow,
but then it abandoned me to find my own way round the
western slopes of Snaefell. The Ordnance Survey marked
the route as 'undefined' on the map, and they were right.
Miles of open hillside stretched ahead, and although there
was no trace of a path, the view was superb. On my left I
could look down to the deep cleft of Sulby Glen and over
the coastal plain to the sea at Jurby. Ahead on the horizon
the shapely dome of North Barrule guided me in the
direction of Ramsey.

After an hour of passing through what appeared to be
firm ground, it turned out to be well-camouflaged bog,
and a lot of time was wasted searching for another way.
Thor and Lucy were dripping with sweat as I was forced
higher and higher up Snaefell in an attempt to avoid the
bogs, and when a line of coaches on the mountain railway
clanked into view climbing slowly towards the summit, I
realized I had strayed a long way off my route. Through
the binoculars I could see what appeared to be a signpost
and a gate far below at the edge of a river, and I headed
for them.

Descending was much easier on the ponies and, apart
from a few anxious moments when Lucy nose-dived into a
patch of soft moss and had to be pulled out, we managed
to avoid the worst places and reach the signpost. But our

troubles were by no means over. There was a steep drop to the river and, worst of all, what had looked like a gate was in fact a stile, and nothing short of Pegasus could have got over it. Tethering Thor to the signpost, I led Lucy carefully down the bank to the river and leapt from boulder to boulder, pulling her gently through the water behind me. With a final bound she reached the other side, and I let her graze while I went back to retrieve Thor. Though I searched up and down the fence for almost an hour, there was no sign of a gate and, returning to the ponies, I brewed a cup of coffee on the paraffin stove and sat by the river working out what I should do.

'If this is the ancient Royal Way,' I complained to Lucy, angrily hurling stones into the water, 'the bloody kings must have travelled along it on horseback, so why the hell put a stile instead of a gate?'

She looked sympathetic, but there were more important things on her mind – Thor had found a patch of fresh grass, and she went off to investigate. Examining the stile, I discovered that the ends of the wire fence were not stapled to the post but wound loosely round it. With the aid of pliers it took only a few minutes to open the fence, lead the ponies through, and fasten the wire securely again. Studying the ground ahead, I had a feeling that we had gone from the frying pan into the fire. The slope was gentle enough, but the whole hillside appeared to be a wide expanse of bog, and there was no alternative but to go through it. Hobbling the ponies, I walked ahead and immediately sank over my boots in the mire. I scouted around and marked out what seemed to be a fairly safe route and, leading Lucy forward, I left Thor to follow. The ground trembled with every step as we squelched cautiously through the bog, but we would have got through without incident had it not been for Thor. Normally when I lead Lucy over a bad patch, he follows as if glued to her tail, but on this occasion he decided he did not trust my judgement and would choose his own way. It was only when I heard gasping and splashing that I turned to find the silly old fool had tried to walk through the softest, slimiest, most horrible patch of bog to be found and had promptly sunk into it like a stone.

A horse in a bog is not a happy sight. They get themselves into a terrible panic, and the frantic heaving and struggling only cause them to sink even further into the churned up mess, until, if the bog is deep enough, they disappear altogether. Thor had gone down as far as his knees, though by the noise he was making he had obviously convinced himself he was about to meet his maker.

'Serves you right, you brainless idiot!' I shouted. 'No Fell pony in his right mind would have gone through there. You're a disgrace!'

His shrill, pathetic whinny implored me to pull him out, and he lurched forward in a desperate bid to get free.

'Hold on a minute,' I growled. 'Keep still while I get a rope on you.' I carried a long rope for such emergencies and, clipping it on his head collar, I tied the end to the pack saddle. With Lucy straining forward, the rope tightened and Thor rose from the bog in a whirl of hooves and sticky mud.

Beyond the danger area the ground was dry and safe, and the ponies walked easily up to join a well-worn path a few yards from the main road, marked on the map as East Mountain Gate. Looking back the way we had come, I was alarmed to see a wide bank of black cloud approaching from the south. It was as if a roller blind was being pulled over the island, shutting out more and more of the blue sky until finally it engulfed the sun and the colours faded from the hills. A few heavy spots of rain warned of worse to come, and I barely had time to pull my waterproofs on before a deluge poured down as if it had been squirted from a mammoth soda syphon. Within minutes the surface of the path was churned into a quagmire, and I was worried that the ponies might put a foot into a concealed hole. In parts the path was so deeply rutted by motor-cycle wheels and the eroding action of water that a slip could easily have resulted in a broken leg. To add to the discomfort, the rain condensing on the warm ground rose in a thick mist, and Lucy was only a vague shadow behind Thor.

From East Mountain Gate the path ran alongside a wall

for a while before turning off and dropping downhill to cross a wide, flat plateau. On all sides there were hills, and over the centuries water had drained off them and transformed the plateau into a lake of soft peat moss and bog myrtle. Somewhere in the middle of it was the Millennium Way.

When I halted at the edge and stared through the rain in the hope of spotting a guide post, it looked an impossible place for ponies. With the aid of a stick I found lying in a ditch, I prodded around until I worked out what I hoped was a passable route, and marked it with a line of digestive biscuits. I was reluctant to waste food, but the biscuits showed up well in the mist, and it was with the unwitting assistance of Messrs McVitie & Price that the ponies splashed safely through that awful place and we rejoined the Millennium Way on higher ground.

The heavy rain eased off as we reached the top of a hill and for a brief moment the sun broke gloriously through, sending a shaft of light down Glen Auldyn and across the glistening rooftops of Ramsey in the far distance. But it was only a teaser, and the rain returned and drummed on the hood of my jacket as relentlessly as ever.

Dropping down to a gate, we left the bleak hillside behind, and continued on down Sky Hill along a broad, grass-covered track flanked by stone walls. The ponies were hungry and kept stopping to snatch at the grass, but I pushed them on until we reached the edge of a wood where I was able to shelter under the trees and heat a pan of soup. Holding the mug of hot soup restored the circulation to my wet hands, and sheltered by a large tree I lay back and listened to the ponies munching the grass and shaking themselves vigorously to get rid of the rain. Some believe that there was once a fairy settlement on the summit of Sky Hill, though after the Vikings fought a furious battle on the spot the little people may well have moved to a quieter neighbourhood!

Of all the generations of Viking warriors who invaded the Isle of Man, the one who carved his name deepest in the island's history was Godred Crovan, son of Harold the

Black of Iceland. While King of Dublin in 1076, Godred turned his expansionist eye towards Man, but the natives were more than a match for his army and forced the invaders to retreat to their boats and row hard for Ireland. Angered by the blow to his pride, he assembled a larger force and attacked the island again. Once more the islanders sent him packing, and Godred slunk away to Dublin to study his combat manuals. By 1079 he had worked out his strategy, and one dark night, in true commando style, he landed 300 men on the beach near Ramsey and hid them in a wood on Sky Hill. When daylight came and the Manx people saw Viking ships sailing into Ramsey Bay, the alarm was raised and the invaders received a hot reception. In the midst of the fierce battle, when it seemed the Manx were about to win the day, the 300 men swooped down from Sky Hill and joined in the fray. Finding themselves out-manoeuvred, the Manx were forced to surrender.

With a compassion uncharacteristic of a Viking conqueror, Godred ordered his army to spare the defeated islanders and allowed them to settle in the north of the island. He gave his own men the choice of either settling permanently or plundering what they could and returning home. To most of them the excitement of plunder was a more attractive proposition than scratching a living from the land, and filling their boats with loot they rowed away to haggle with the Dublin pawnbrokers. Pleased to be rid of the hotheads in his army, Godred gave the fertile southern half of the island to those who remained with him, and he made an attempt at stabilizing the island by writing out a constitution and establishing the first legislative body. Now that he was King of Man as well as Dublin and the Hebrides, Godred's three sons, Lagman, Harald and Olaf, helped him to maintain a tight control over his realms.

In Viking history life was never peaceful for very long, and in Norway the ambitious King Magnus was poring over maps and drawing lines round Scotland and the Isle of Man. He set sail with a large army and conquered the Hebrides, capturing Godred's son Lagman and joining

forces with the King of Leinster to unseat Godred Crovan
from the throne of Dublin. The unfortunate Godred was
chased from pillar to post and died a disillusioned man on
the island of Islay in 1095.

Had he lived another three years, Godred would have
been saddened to hear of civil war in his beloved Isle of
Man. Magnus of Norway, who was then ruler of the
Hebrides, was busy warring elsewhere, and the Vikings
who had settled in the south of the island after Godred's
battle on Sky Hill took advantage of his absence to pick a
fight with the Manx who lived in the north. The two sides
fought each other in a pitched battle near Peel, and the
southerners soon discovered they had taken on more than
they had bargained for. The natives came armed with a
powerful natural force the Vikings had never before
encountered: Manx women were fighting alongside their
men. The Vikings were completely bewildered! To them,
women were creature-comforts to help pass the time
between long voyages. To be faced with lopping a female
head off in battle was an uncomfortable experience, and
while they hesitated, the women settled old scores with an
axe. The northerners won the day. But their glory was
short-lived. Mighty Magnus sailed into Peel with a fleet of
ships fresh from a campaign to subdue clan risings in the
Hebrides, and liked the fertile island so much he built a
fort and used it as a base until, in true Viking style, he
himself fell in battle fighting the Irish.

While I was day-dreaming in the shelter of the tree, Lucy
had taken Thor and wandered back up the track to
investigate a grass patch by the gate. Cursing myself for
not having used the hobbles, I hastily bundled the stove
into its box and trudged up the hill after them. Thor stood
silently while I ranted and raved, but Lucy stuck her nose
in the air with a supercilious expression and chewed a
mouthful of grass in defiance. I gave them a mint to make
friends again, and we continued on our way down Sky
Hill.

There was absolutely no let-up in the rain, but it was
such a pleasure to ride along a good track enjoying the

aroma of the spruce trees and listening to the chatter of a flock of magpies that I hardly noticed it. The delights of the ride through the wood ended all too soon when the track dipped down to a cluster of farm buildings and joined a busy main road. While I was adjusting the packs, a man standing in the doorway of one of the buildings strolled over and stood eyeing the ponies. He walked first to one side, then the other, looked at their teeth and feet, then stood back, scratching his head under his cap and sucking his teeth noisily. He looked every inch a horse-dealer.

'These are Fells, aren't they?' he said at last.

'Yes,' I said. 'They're both registered Fells.'

'H'm,' he said, rubbing his chin thoughtfully. 'Pack pony's a bit on the light side, but this feller's well built.' He patted Thor's rump, then, reaching for his hip pocket, he said briskly: 'How much would you take for 'em?'

'I'm not selling them,' I laughed. 'They're worth more to me than money!'

'Come on,' he urged. 'Everyone's got their price.'

'Not where these two are concerned,' I said. 'You can forget it!'

Pushing the wallet back in his pocket, he smiled and said, 'I don't blame you, but I often think we sometimes go soft in the head over hosses. They get more fuss and attention than we do.' He went on to tell me he had been running a pony-trekking centre on the island for a number of years, but he was on the point of selling up. 'There aren't the folk about these days,' he said sadly. 'I remember the time when I could have kept twenty or more hosses working every day during the summer, but nowadays it's as cheap for the holidaymakers to spend a week in Spain as it is here.'

'How will the island survive if the visitors stop coming?' I asked.

'Damned if I know,' he said. 'All sorts of things have been tried to provide jobs for the youngsters, but they don't last long. The future for them isn't very bright.' Rain dripped onto the end of his nose, and he blew it off in a cloud of spray and dried his face with his coat sleeve.

'Opportunities for getting on have always been few and far between on the island,' he went on. 'It always reminds me of the story of a fishing boat coming into Ramsey harbour one day with a load of crabs. While a crowd of visitors was watching them unload, one of the crabs crawled over the edge of the box and was setting off along the quay when a fisherman put his boot on it.

' "That's cruel!" shouts one of the visitors.

' "Oh, I don't know," says the fisherman, "It's true Manx, that crab. Just when it thought it was getting on in the world, some sod tramples all over it!" '

He was about to launch into another story when a sudden increase in the rain sent him scampering back to the farm.

'The forecast is better for tomorrow,' he shouted over his shoulder. 'I think we're in for a hot spell.'

'I hope you're right,' I shouted back, pulling the ponies under the shelter of a large sycamore. 'If it rains much more, I'll grow webbed feet!'

The extra burst of rain turned out to be a final gesture from the clouds as they sailed on towards Scotland, and within half an hour the rain had stopped and patches of blue sky began to appear.

I had arranged to camp at Grenaby Farm, about five miles north of Ramsey, and the map showed a track crossing the Sulby river at a ford, which would save having to take the ponies through the town. I found the track easily enough, but when I reached the ford, the river was swollen with floodwater. Fortunately the local council had erected a footbridge, but to get Lucy across I had to raise the packs to clear the handrails. It took only a few minutes to organize, but a military-looking man, sporting a bristly moustache and leading a dog, stamped his walking-stick impatiently as he waited to cross on the other side. Coaxing Lucy gently over the bridge, with Thor following on his own, I was about to apologize to the man for holding him up when he barked, 'Can't you read?'

'I'm sorry. I don't know what you mean!' I said, taken aback by his aggressive manner.

'Perhaps you are one of those people who believe that

notices are not intended for them,' he snapped. 'If you would care to read this,' – he rapped a sign with his stick – 'it states quite plainly "Pedestrians only".'

'Well, I'm sorry. I didn't see a notice,' I said, 'but in any case the river is in spate and I daren't risk taking the ponies through the ford.'

'That is not the point,' he snapped. 'Instructions are to be obeyed! Now kindly remove those animals so that I can pass.'

Still standing on the bridge, Thor chose the wrong time to relieve himself. Lifting his tail, he let fall a heap of steaming droppings. For a moment the man could hardly believe his eyes: 'Look at that,' he roared, pointing at the heap. 'This has gone too far! I shall report it to the authorities immediately. You damned gypsies can't do as you like, you know.'

That taunt really riled me, and I flung Lucy's lead rope furiously to the ground. The man grabbed his dog and scurried away along the river bank.

'Report it to who the hell you want, you pompous twit!' I yelled after him. I was shaking with rage and, dragging the bewildered Thor off the bridge, I kicked the droppings into the river.

'You don't want to let those wheneyes upset you,' said a man's voice from behind a hedge as I led the ponies past one of the smart houses near the river.

'Those what?' I said, peering through the branches.

'Wheneyes,' repeated the voice. 'Think they own the world, they do, but they're nobody really. The chap who was on at you by the bridge is typical of the breed.' I still could not see the man behind the hedge, and it was a strange experience talking to a detached voice.

'Why do you call them "wheneyes"?' I asked.

'Oh, it's 'cos most of 'em lived abroad before they retired to the island, and to show off they always start a conversation with, "When I was in India" or "When I was in Africa", or "When I was ..." wherever they happen to have been. If you get a few of 'em talking together, it's hilarious. That's why locals call 'em "wheneyes". They're not all as bad as the one you met. Some of them are quite nice people, but they can't get used to the idea that they aren't dealing with natives any more.' A telephone in the house started to ring, and the voice said, 'You'll have to excuse me. Enjoy your journey! I read about you in the local paper.'

I felt terribly conspicuous as I rode between the rows of houses, each with its well-trimmed lawn and air of comfortable affluence. Here and there a net curtain twitched as the occupants strained to get a closer look at the unusual spectacle passing their doors. One lady was bold enough to smile and wave at me from a bedroom window, and I blew her a kiss in the best cavalier style. It was only when I looked down that I found myself staring into the tight-lipped face of her husband, busy clipping the garden hedge.

Given the choice, I would rather struggle a dozen miles over rough, mountainous country than go half that distance along a flat tarmac road, but travelling north from Ramsey there is no alternative. When the glaciers landscaped the north of the island, they left it flat and fertile, which pleased the farmers, but the old tracks which bounded the farms were eventually surfaced and classified as roads, and horse-riders are obliged to share them with motor vehicles.

Away from Ramsey, with its aggressive colonials and well-ordered urban respectability, I was able to relax and, with the sun on my back and the ponies jogging steadily along, we followed the black ribbon of road running parallel with the coast. After grey skies and rain the warmth of the sun had a magical effect on the countryside. There was a fragrance of soil and grass lingering in the air, and the newly washed landscape was a colourful mixture of attractive farmhouses and cottages, green fields and dark woods edged with the blue of the sea where the long sweep of the coastline reached towards the Point of Ayre.

There was a lot of traffic on the road but the drivers were very considerate, slowing down as they approached and giving a friendly wave as they drove by. At least, they all did with the exception of the blonde bombshell ...

We had turned inland from the coast at the village of

Dog Mills to follow a minor road to Grenaby Farm and had gone only a mile or so when a blonde girl driving a sports car came roaring up behind, sounding the horn impatiently for us to move over. Without waiting for me to pull the ponies to one side, she attempted to get through by driving onto the grass verge, and immediately one wheel sank to its hubcap in the soft ground. Flinging the car door open, she heaved herself out in a frenzy of suntanned legs, pale blue dress and long blonde hair.

'Damn and blast!' she cursed, kicking the half buried wheel. 'Damn and blast! I'm going to be late picking Daddy up at the airport. He'll be furious!'

I walked over and looked at the wheel. It was well down in the mud, but the other three were on hard ground. With the aid of a small folding spade I carried in Lucy's pack, a few bricks lying in the grass, and me pushing on the rear bumper while the blonde kept the wheels turning with the engine, we got the car back on the road and she was overjoyed.

'Thanks a million,' she said, revving the engine and eager to be on her way. 'Is there any way I can help you?'

On the windscreen of the car was a sticker that said, 'Young Farmers Do It In Wellies.' 'I don't think so,' I said, 'but that's an interesting invitation on your windscreen. Would I be eligible in climbing boots?'

She looked at the sticker and started to laugh. 'I'm afraid not, but thanks for your help anyway. 'Bye.'

With a roar the sports car shot away down the road, spattering me with mud. Thor and Lucy looked up from where they had been grazing, and I could have sworn they were trying hard not to laugh.

'Laugh your silly heads off if it makes you feel any better!' I said, scraping a lump of mud off my face and flinging it onto the road. 'Women are like that. You can't win 'em all.'

We arrived at Grenaby in the late afternoon, and farmer John Huyton and his wife Sandra were very welcoming. The ponies were given the run of a twenty-acre field. At the sight of grass they went wild with excitement and tore round and round at full gallop like a pair of yearlings.

Thor slowed down, blowing with exertion as he passed the gate, but Lucy whinnied at him and with a flick of her head galloped across the field again. When Thor sets off at speed, it is like watching a heavily laden Jumbo Jet taking off. There is a series of short lumbering bounces before lift-off, but it is always an economy flight. He never lifts his feet higher than the very minimum needed to achieve forward motion. I left them enjoying a blissful roll in the grass and went back to the farm.

The Huytons had other guests staying and, having succumbed to the offer of a hot bath, a chance to dry my wet clothes, and a bed in the farmhouse, I went down for the evening meal to find I was sharing a table with a very smartly dressed couple who had arrived in a Rolls-Royce. They were Susan and Peter Harris-Bates from Dover, and not the least bit affected by owning a superior motor car, though throughout the meal I was very conscious of my left elbow protruding through a hole in the sleeve of my sweater and an aroma of horse sweat which no amount of deodorant, talcum powder, body lotion or the mystical concoctions of Chanel could overcome.

It was a perfect summer evening with a warm sun shining down from a cloudless sky, and after dinner I took my friends to meet Thor and Lucy, and they in turn introduced me to the Rolls. Peter's hobby was restoring vintage cars, and the colour photographs he showed me of cars he had owned would have stirred envy in the heart of any car-enthusiast. The Rolls was fairly new and stood smugly in the muddy farmyard with its immaculate paintwork glinting in the sun, and while I could appreciate Peter's immense pride in owning the King of Motor Cars, to me it was like a fearsomely expensive show-jumping horse or a racing yacht – the ultimate for special occasions but not very practical and a bit ostentatious for everyday use. These were the thoughts of a philistine, and I kept them to myself!

'It's fascinating that you are touring the island on horseback while we're touring in a Rolls,' said Peter, carefully closing the bonnet after showing me the gleaming engine. 'How would you like to go from one extreme to the other and come for a drive? We're going to the Point of Ayre.'

I was touched with a pang of conscience about leaving the ponies while I wallowed in luxury, but consoled myself with the thought that twenty acres of grass all to themselves was just as indulgent, and I sank back into the soft leather of the front seat to watch the countryside swish by as the car purred effortlessly along the narrow roads.

Motor cars are something I've never been madly excited about, but the Rolls was certainly in a class of its own. Everything about it was designed to relieve the owner of any form of physical effort, and there were so many push-buttons set into the polished walnut fascia panel that I felt that if I pressed the wrong one while trying to adjust my seat I might be catapulted through the roof, like a scene from a James Bond film. Peter demonstrated the air-conditioning system, and the temperature in the car ranged from sweltering hot to teeth-chattering cold in seconds. It was a vast improvement on the fug-stirrers that pass for heaters in the average family saloon, but the unit was so complicated it needed a car the size of the Rolls to carry it.

I might have enjoyed the ride more had I not felt some discomfort about the attention the car attracted. People standing at cottage gates and outside village pubs turned to stare as the car went by, and I was never sure if I should give a royal wave and a gracious smile or ignore the attention and concentrate on the road ahead. As we were passing through St Bride, a group of children stopped their game when the Rolls approached, and as we reached them the girls curtsied and the boys bowed. It was all done in fun, but in their great-grandfathers' day it would have been expected of them when any 'gentry' went by.

Susan wanted to watch the sun setting over the sea from the Point of Ayre lighthouse, and we pulled into a parking space alongside a battered Citroën covered in CND and Peace stickers. Our arrival interrupted the passionate embraces of a young couple sat in the front, and they hurriedly disentangled themselves and stared coldly up at the Rolls and me. I smiled and waved, but they made no response.

'Toffee-nosed bugger,' I heard the lad say to the girl. 'I bet he's never done a day's work in his life. He's the sort who hasn't a clue about the real issues affecting the world.'

'Yeah,' agreed the girl. 'Just a wealthy creep with no concern for anyone but himself. Let's get out of here.'

As the Citroën drove away, the girl flung a handful of sandwich wrappers and paper cups out of the car window, and they scattered in an unsightly mess over the grass. A large sign in the rear of the car said, 'Make the world a better place to live in.'

We watched in silence as the setting sun streaked the western horizon in an ever-changing kaleidoscope of green, purple, red and gold, before sinking gently into the sea. As darkness descended, the shore, the sea and the sky merged into a vast emptiness, illuminated briefly by flashes of light as the powerful beam revolved at the top of the lighthouse. Except for the cry of an oyster-catcher and the occasional rumble of shingle on the beach as a wave broke over it there was not a sound and when Peter started the car to drive back to Grenaby the noise seemed to reverberate across the island.

5

Lucy goes Lame, Thor goes Solo

A cock crowing outside my bedroom window woke me early the next morning, and I looked out over a dew-soaked orchard with wispy strands of mist draped over the trees like silver thread. The weatherman on the radio promised a dry day with a light sea breeze, and by nine o'clock the dew and mist had evaporated and the sky was clear. The sea breeze arrived as forecast, but what the weatherman forgot to mention was that it had passed over the Polar ice-cap on its way to the Isle of Man, and the temperature was decidedly chilly.

It took me ages to find the ponies. John had left all the field gates open after getting his silage crop in, and with a hundred acres to wander over, Lucy would have insisted on tasting the grass in every field. I felt I had walked all the way back to Ramsey before I found them leaning over a hedge in earnest conversation with an old carthorse on the next farm. There was an air of conspiracy in the way they stood muzzle to muzzle, listening while the carthorse snickered and squealed as if trying to persuade them that, if only they would join his campaign for the liberation of working horses, they would be freed from the bondage of carrying the pack saddle and me and could lie in the sun all day. Lucy hesitated for a second or two when I whistled, then trotted over to me, but Thor's head was full of the promise of a life of blissful idleness, and each time I attempted to slip a halter over his head he shied away, kicking his hind legs triumphantly in the air, while the carthorse snorted his approval over the hedge.

'Please yourself,' I called out as he pranced round the field. 'You can stay here for ever if that's what you want.'

Slowly and deliberately I peeled the wrapper off a stick of barley sugar and made a great fuss of feeding it to Lucy in tantalizing lumps. Thor watched enviously as she crunched each piece, and the bursts of high-spirited bucking gradually subsided as it dawned on him that there were certain disadvantages in being liberated. Abandoning the carthorse and freedom, he caught up with us as I was leading Lucy into the farmyard. Peter Harris-Bates helped me carry the saddles and bags out of the barn, and within half an hour the ponies were loaded and I was waving goodbye as we made our way down the farm lane. We had almost reached the road when John Huyton started to run after us.

'Hey, stop a minute,' he shouted. 'The pack pony is lame in one leg.' I pulled Thor up abruptly and slid out of the saddle.

'Lame?' I said, as John reached me. 'She can't be lame! I've just checked her feet in the yard and she was fine.'

'Well, she's not fine now,' answered John tersely. 'Watch while I walk her up the lane.'

Grabbing Lucy's lead rope, he led her back towards the house. I could hardly believe it! Not only was she limping, she was positively stumbling on her nearside hind leg, and it was obvious she was in considerable pain. She winced as I carefully lifted the leg to see if a stone had lodged in her shoe and, though there was no stone, the fetlock area above her hoof was hot and swollen. It was a sure sign of injury, and there was no question of Lucy being able to continue the journey until it had recovered.

'Isn't that just my rotten luck?' I said wearily to John as he helped me lead the ponies back into the yard. 'I've spent months planning this journey, and now after three days it looks as if I'll have to abandon it and take Lucy home. I still can't understand how it happened – she was rushing about like a foal this morning!'

'Oh, it could have happened any time,' said John. 'Maybe she banged it on a rock when you came over the hills and it only started to bother her when she set off this morning.' He paused, deep in thought for a moment or two. 'Look,' he said, 'there's no need to abandon your journey. You're welcome to leave her here if you can manage with one pony for a day or two. I'll get the vet to look at her; I'm sure it's not serious!'

I could have shouted with relief. 'It'll be a tremendous help, John. I can't thank you enough.'

'That's OK,' he smiled. 'Leave any gear you don't want in the barn and get on your way.'

Thor stood patiently while I adjusted the pack saddle to his broad back and loaded the packs on but, the moment I led him away from the farm and he realized we had left Lucy behind, he refused to go on.

'Keep moving, you silly old fool!' I bellowed, heaving on his lead rope in exasperation. 'Until Lucy is better you're carrying the pack and I'm walking, so let's go!'

It felt as if I was towing an elephant as we made our way slowly along the road. Lucy made the situation worse by answering his calls and, as the pitiful whinnying echoed across the fields, passers-by began to give me odd looks, as if they suspected I might be a horse-thief. Even when Lucy was finally out of earshot Thor kept up the din, and it was most embarrassing passing through Bride village with people leaning over garden hedges demanding to know what was wrong with 'the poor little pony'. I did my best to explain the situation, but few seemed convinced, and others went away muttering about police and the RSPCA. Salvation came in the form of council refuse lorries, which banged and clattered along the road to a tip near the Point of Ayre. The lorries were nicely spaced out, so that each time Thor was about to launch into one of his whinnying spectaculars, a lorry would appear and drown the noise.

The lighthouse car-park was packed with visitors, and the pain of parting with Lucy was soon forgotten. Within seconds he was the centre of attention as swarms of little girls and mums rushed to pat his nose and feed him pieces of chocolate and sweets. As always, he played to the gallery with a convincing performance of an old and neglected, half-starved, unloved pony with a sadistic owner who forced him to carry heavy loads. With sad brown eyes he stood dejectedly appealing to his audience, and they fell for it. He was magnificent in his deception. The great tragedian, the Laurence Olivier of ponies. It was ages before I managed to pull him away and hide him in a clump of gorse bushes while I photographed the lighthouse.

I have been fascinated by lighthouses since I was a boy and worked as a deckhand on a fishing vessel trawling off the west coast of Scotland. One morning in summer, as we steamed out of a thick mist into a sunlit patch south of the Isle of Mull, there, rising out of the sea on a plinth of foaming white breakers, was the tall grey tower of Skerryvore lighthouse. It was the most wonderful sight I had ever seen and, though I have sailed past it many times since, I never cease to marvel at the beauty of its architecture and the courage of the men who built it.

There can be few people who are not familiar with the poetry and stories of Robert Louis Stevenson, but by his father and uncles Robert was looked upon as a failure in a family of engineers with a reputation as the greatest lighthouse-builders of all time. The Stevensons were engineers to the Northern Lighthouse Board in Edinburgh, and established their reputation as lighthouse-builders when Robert Louis's grandfather built a lighthouse on the notorious Bell Rock on Scotland's east coast. Most of the time the rock was covered by the sea, yet somehow Robert Stevenson and his men built a huge granite tower on it. Each granite block was dovetailed to fit the adjoining one like a jigsaw puzzle, and tapered on its outside edge – all done by masons using nothing more than a mallet and chisel. It was an incredible feat, and it led to more work designing and building lighthouses around Scotland's coast.

Civil servants in Westminster have never quite understood the independence of the Isle of Man, and in 1815 they were obviously not familiar with its geographical position either and put the island's lighthouses under the control of the Scottish-based Northern Lighthouse Board.

In the event the island benefited enormously from the Stevensons' skill and experience, and they lost no time in building lighthouses at the Point of Ayre and the Calf of Man.

By 1832 another new light was flashing a warning from the top of Douglas Head but, fully occupied with building other lighthouses, including Skerryvore, forty years or more passed before the Stevensons returned to the island to construct their architectural gem on the Chicken Rock. After almost twenty years of arguments with stubborn officials in London, the Northern Lighthouse Board finally convinced them that lives would be saved by a lighthouse on Langness, and the light was lit for the first time in December 1880. The last of the island's monuments to several generations of engineering genius guides ships round Maughold Head.

At the Point of Ayre one of the keepers was about to take a party of four elderly Irish ladies and a priest up the tower as I arrived in the yard, so I followed at a discreet distance as they puffed and wheezed their way up the narrow spiral stone staircase. The keeper led the way, with the priest and three of his charges close on his heels, but the fourth, large and well-endowed, was having a hard time lifting her heavy frame up the steps, and she soon fell behind. As I caught up with her, she sank to her knees with a groan and clung to the handrail, her eyes closed.

'Holy Mother of God!' she gasped. 'I can't go on! Me old heart's done for.'

'Bridget, are you all right down there?' The soft voice of the priest drifted down the tower with a celestial echo, and the old lady looked startled until she realized who it was.

'Did you hear that now? Yer man fancies he's the angel Gabriel himself!' she hissed. Then in a louder voice, 'I'm fine, Father. Just resting. I'll be with you in a minute.'

I helped her to her feet and she gripped the handrail to heave herself up the steps.

'Bejaysus, I'll tell you something,' she whispered, looking cautiously up the tower to make sure the priest was out of earshot. 'If the steps up to the pearly gates yer man's always preaching about are as bad as these, then I'd rather go down and keep company with the Devil!'

At the top of the steps eager hands helped her into a small room below the lantern, and she sank onto a stool.

'Congratulations, Bridget,' beamed the priest. '107 steps if I'm not mistaken. You'll get to Heaven yet!'

'Well, if it's all the same to you, Father,' said the old lady innocently, 'the next time we go on an outing maybe we can visit a cave.' She looked across at me with a twinkle in her eye. 'I'm just after telling yer man here that it can be a lot warmer when you go down!'

Thankfully the priest missed the point.

'To be sure, it's chilly up here, right enough,' he said gently. 'We'll have a quick look at the lantern, ladies, then we'll go back to the coach.'

Choking back a fit of laughter, I pushed through a door and escaped onto the outside balcony.

The wind coming in off the sea was bitterly cold, but the view was superb. The Cumberland coast to the east and the Irish coast to the west were lost in haze, but to the north the Mull of Galloway and the Scottish coast were so near it looked as though it might be possible to walk across when the tide was out.

There were many times when, as far as the villagers of Bride and the surrounding district were concerned, Scotland was too close for comfort. With only sixteen miles of sea separating the island from Galloway, the prosperous farms and villages around the Point of Ayre were fair game for the Scots raiders, and they paid frequent visits. They would wait until smoke could be seen coming from the farm chimneys, a sign that a meal was being prepared, then they would hop into their boats and arrive in time for dinner.

For centuries Manx people believed that, through the action of the sea piling shingle on the beach, the Point of Ayre was slowly extending towards Scotland. It was prophesied that the time would come when the Manx people would be able to walk to Scotland – or, put more succinctly by one ancient sorceress: 'The Manx and the Scotch will come so near as to throw their beetles at each other.' When someone pointed out that, at the time the lighthouse was built in 1818 it was on the extreme point but since then the sea had retreated and the tower was now a considerable distance inland, the possibility of an Isle of Man versus Scotland beetle-throwing competition loomed larger, but a Manx worthy spoilt it by writing to the Northern Lighthouse Board, who sent a detailed specification of the original site, with measurements proving that very little change had in fact taken place.

When I returned to the tower, the priest and the ladies had gone, and the keeper was waiting to lock up. He gave me a rapid tour of the lantern room and a demonstration of the revolving mechanism, then I was whisked downstairs and out into the yard.

At first sight the Ayres, the five or six miles of shoreline running down the west side of the island towards Blue Point, looks flat and uninteresting; but it is deceptive. In geological jargon it is a raised beach formed in post-glacial times, but in reality it is a delightful combination of polished shingle, close-cropped heather, white sand, marram grass and the most fascinating variety of wild flowers to be found anywhere on the island. Arctic terns, oyster-catchers and gulls of all shapes and sizes filled the air, screaming with indignation if Thor's large feet thumped down close to their nests.

'What a nice little pony,' said the woman at the National Trust information centre patronizingly, 'but these native breeds are pretty useless for hard work. You really ought to use Arabs for this sort of journey. They never need shoeing, you know.'

I wanted to tell her about the hundreds of miles Thor had covered, over mountains and through bogs, in gales, rain and snow, that he was also the kindest and most lovable pony I had ever owned and that, as for Arab horses never needing shoeing – I had never listened to such utter rubbish! But I said nothing; I concentrated on removing an imaginary stone from one of Thor's shoes, and when I looked up, she had gone.

Beyond the National Trust information centre the easy surface of the Ayres ended, and we had to pick our way through tall sand dunes and thick clumps of marram grass. Weighed down by the heavy packs, Thor continually sank up to his knees in the soft sand, and he was soon lathered in sweat. I studied the map, trying to decide if I should relieve the strain on Thor by turning inland to reach a road, but at Rue Point the decision was made for me by a wire fence which barred the way and forced us to scramble down onto the beach and follow the edge of the sea. Underfoot it alternated between soft sand and loose shingle, and after an hour Thor was so exhausted he could hardly stay on his feet, but there was no sign of a suitable place to stop for the night. Fresh water flowing out of the Lhen Trench onto the beach provided him with a welcome drink, and I rested for a while to let him cool off. The wide mouth of the Trench looked like the entrance to an inland canal, but in fact it was no more than an enormous ditch cut through six miles of countryside to drain the Curraghs, a large expanse of boggy ground between Ballaugh and Sulby.

South of the Lhen Trench the shoreline rose in a series of weathered cliffs of red clay called 'The Brews', which looked very attractive in the late-afternoon sun but seemed so impregnable I began to worry that we might be trapped by the incoming tide. The beach was endless, and we plodded mechanically on, splashing through pools of water and crunching over long, monotonous beds of shingle, until a cluster of concrete buildings came into view, shimmering in a haze at the foot of the cliffs. I thought at first it was a mirage, but they were real enough. Hitching Thor's lead rope to a metal ball lodged in the sand, I raced ahead to find shelter for the night.

It was a dreadful place. Whether the buildings had once been part of a quarry or a wartime gun-emplacement, it was difficult to judge. Years of neglect, helped by countless gales driving sand and shingle into every opening, had reduced them to a jungle of shattered concrete and rusty metal. Crude graffiti, empty beer cans and motor-cycle tracks were everywhere, and the whole place had a Wild West ghost-town atmosphere about it. It had such a feeling of evil it might well have been the lair of a modern band of Carrasdhoo men, a villainous gang of robbers who terrorized the west of the island in the eighteenth century. Their hide-out was an ale house deep in the Curragh, where they made a tidy living from robbing their guests and dumping their bodies in the bog. No one knows how many unfortunate travellers disappeared in this way.

> There lay a hut by a lone wayside
> A publican's hovel, but woe betide
> The wretch whom thirst or weariness led
> Into the dark pestiferous shed,
> For to drink there once was to drink no more
> And there came no tales from the dark trap door.

The chilling lines come from a poem by Esther Nelson, a clergyman's daughter, which is based on the story of how the Carrasdhoo men robbed and murdered an Irish pedlar boy and threw his body in the Curragh bog. News of the crime leaked out but, though there is no record of the gang's being convicted, nothing more is heard of them.

Returning to Thor, I was amused to find that the metal ball I had tethered him to was a World War II mine that had washed up at some time and been de-fused and left to rot. Even had it been live and gone off with a bang, I doubt if he would have noticed: he was stretched out on the sand fast asleep, pack saddle and all, snoring peacefully. I felt a heel having to wake him, but evening was fast approaching and I still had to find a way up the cliffs, and a campsite for the night.

The tide had come in high up the beach, and for a while I detoured round it, but struggling through the wet sand was so laborious that it was easier and more refreshing to splash through the breakers. We had walked about two miles when I spied a wide gully between the cliffs and a path leading to Sartfield. It was steep and loose but Thor bravely scrambled up, and when we emerged at the top I could hardly believe my luck! We were in a field and about half a mile away was a farm.

Leaving Thor tied to a fence post gulping the grass, I

walked up to the farm to ask if I could camp but though I could hear voices in the house, no amount of hammering on the back door brought a response. I tried the front door, but it was overgrown with weeds and ivy and obviously hadn't been opened in years. I hammered on the back door again, and this time I heard footsteps clattering through the stone kitchen. The door was flung open and an old man eyed me suspiciously.

'We're not buying anything! Who are you?' he growled.

'It's all right,' I laughed. 'I'm not a salesman. I'm touring the island with a pony and wondered if I could camp for the night on the cliff top.'

'Travelling with a pony?' he said, looking puzzled. 'Where is it?' He walked out into the yard and I pointed to Thor's shadowy figure at the end of the field, nose down, scarcely pausing for breath as he cropped the grass around the fence post. 'Bonny little animal,' said the farmer. 'I'll maybe get a look at him tomorrow. Aye, you can camp. Mind the rabbits don't eat you — there's no shortage of them!' Chuckling at the joke, he walked back into the house and slammed the door.

Thor sank down and rolled in the cool grass when I heaved the packs and saddle off his sweating back, and I was busy unpacking when I heard a car stop in the lane running along the edge of the field. A man got out and walked along the beach for a while, then wandered over, curious to see what I was doing. He produced two cans of beer, and we sat on the cliff top chatting and watching the sun settle slowly towards the sea. To my surprise I discovered that he lived not far from my home in the Lake District and worked for a company installing equipment in a new reservoir scheme below Snaefell.

'How do you find the Manx?' I asked as I leant against a fence post savouring the cool beer.

'Oh, you couldn't find nicer folk anywhere,' he replied. 'They'd give you their last crust, but they're the most frustrating people in the world to work with. They've no idea what the word "urgent" means, and this "never do today what you can put off till tomorrow" way of life plays hell with my work schedule.' He drained the last of the beer and pushed the can into his pocket. 'It's a lovely island, and they're lovely people,' he continued, 'but they will have to come to terms with the inescapable fact that we live in a changing world, and the rustic image of the horse-drawn cart and fairy glens belongs to another age. When I asked one man why it took him twice as long as it should have done to do the easiest of jobs, he said that there was no point in rushing on an island as small as this; if you moved too fast, you could fall into the sea!' He sighed heavily. 'Thank God they're not all as bad as him, but it gives you some idea of what I'm up against.'

The sun had long dipped below the horizon when my friend climbed stiffly to his feet and, wishing me luck, drove off down the lane. Somewhere in the darkness of the field I could hear Thor busily champing through the grass and, burrowing deep into my sleeping-bag, I fell asleep listening to the pounding of the surf on the beach.

6

Bunnies and Bishops

I was wakened in the early hours of the morning by the sound of heavy rain pounding on the tent and, unable to sleep, I lit the paraffin stove and made a pan of coffee. It was very disappointing after the enjoyment of the previous day's sunshine and, peering through the door of the tent at a dull grey sky and a waterlogged landscape, it looked as though the rain had set in for the day.

The farmer was certainly right about there being a lot of rabbits! Myxomatosis has practically wiped out the rabbit population in my part of Cumberland and they are a rare sight, but in the field around the tent there were hundreds of them. When I crept out in my waterproofs to check that Thor had not strayed, there was a flurry of white tails as a stampede of bunnies streaked towards the safety of a gorse-covered mound by the edge of the cliff. Bewildered by the departure of their mums and dads, baby bunnies cowered in the grass, ears flattened along their backs, hoping desperately that the strange hooded creature striding by would not spot them. The amount of grass a rabbit colony can consume in a day is phenomenal, and to see the damage they can inflict on growing crops it is not difficult to appreciate how conflicts can arise between nature, who has a use for rabbits, and farmers, who do not.

The danger is that the conflict can get out of hand when farmers and society in general, through blind ignorance or sheer greed, fail to understand that to upset the balance of nature is to court trouble. When, instead of implementing a carefully thought-out programme for reducing the rabbit population to manageable proportions, the wise men in the Government wantonly unleash a devastating fatal disease on the rabbit population, it violates all the laws of morality and displays a degree of stupidity which is beyond comprehension. Annihilating rabbits leaves foxes and birds of prey without a natural source of food. Their only alternative is to take lambs; so the farmer retaliates by hunting foxes and shooting eagles and falcons. This stirs the anger of the anti-blood-sports supporters and the bird-protectors. So with the blessing of the Ministry of Agriculture, the farmer resorts to a less obtrusive but infinitely more lethal means of getting rid of his lamb-stealers by obtaining strychnine and leaving poisoned carcases in strategic places. As a result foxes and birds die an agonizing death, and in turn their carcases are picked over by crows, farm dogs and family pets, with the same fatal consequences. Strychnine poison never decays; it lies where it is deposited until unearthed by some other unfortunate creature, and the crazy roundabout continues. All because that greatest and most intelligent of animals, *homo sapiens*, sometimes cannot see beyond the end of his nose!

Packing the sodden tent and loading Thor in the pouring rain took longer than usual, and it was mid-morning before we were ready to leave. It would have been easy to drop down onto the beach and continue on our way, but I could not leave without walking the half mile up to Sartfield to thank the farmer. I took Thor with me, and in the yard the farmer stalked round him, head tilted to one side as if he was about to make an offer.

'Aye, I suppose he's all right as hosses go, but I haven't much time for 'em myself.'

'Not much time for them?' I echoed, 'But you seemed keen on horses!'

'Aye, I used to be,' he said, 'but you can't beat a tractor! There was never a horse died that didn't die in debt. Whether it worked or not, it still had to be fed and vetted.'

Having spent my early years on a farm where horses

were used every day and worked very hard, I felt the farmer was being unfair, but there was no point in arguing. There is a breed of farmer who looks on animals as nothing more than breeding-machines or beasts of burden and has very little sentiment for them as enjoyable companions or faithful friends.

It was still raining hard when I left the farm and walked back down the lane to the beach, but visibility was surprisingly good. To the south the scarred nose of Jurby Head jutted out into the sea like a great wall.

Leading Thor through the sand and shingle was as tedious as it had been the previous day, but the monotony was relieved by the dramatic architecture of the cliffs. Rain, wind and waves had sculpted the soft clay into an intricate network of buttresses, arêtes, overhangs and gullies, stretching along the coast as far as the eye could see. Looked at from sea-level, the effect was very beautiful, but the owners of the smart houses dotted along the cliff top would see it only as unrelenting coastal erosion which might one day threaten their property.

Off Jurby Head the beach was strewn with boulders, and lodged among them, half buried in the sand, were the barnacle-encrusted remains of what had once been a sizeable ship. There were no sides or deck to it, just a block of metal barely recognizable as the engine, and a few bleached ribs sticking out from the keel like a discarded fishbone. I poked around to see if I could discover the ship's name, but the wreck kept the secret to itself. It was a sad sight. I wondered where the ship had been bound for on that fateful day when a quirk of fate ended its life on the rocks below Jurby Head.

An agitated snorting and stamping of feet on the shingle told me that Thor was bored standing about in the rain and was impatient to be off. I shared an apple with him while I studied the map to try to identify a tower perched on the cliffs a mile or so down the coast.

There were a lot of aircraft whizzing about in the vicinity of it, and I was worried that we might have strayed into an Air Force bombing range. As it turned out, we had – but fortunately not one where real bombs were used. It was a 'hush-hush' Government establishment with a radar tower and guards on the gates but, apart from two council workmen who had abandoned their grass-mowing activity to drink tea in a portable cabin near the main entrance, no one took the slightest interest in us as I led Thor off the beach to shelter from the weather under a tree. A large sign on the security fence a few yards away warned that by order of the Official Secrets Act we were not to loiter or take photographs, but I hoped that if we were being spied on by the authorities they would allow us to threaten national security at least until the driving rain had eased a little.

We had been there about an hour when a meteorological miracle happened. The rain stopped, the sombre clouds disappeared and the sun beamed down as if the watery interlude had just been one of his little jokes to annoy the forecasters. The warmth of the sun brought the council workers out of their cabin, and they came across to look at Thor and ask where we were going. They were very concerned that I should write about the island as I saw it, and not as if I were writing a tourist brochure.

'If you believed that tourist stuff,' said one of the men, 'you'd think we spent our days dancing around with flowers in our caps or sitting outside a thatched cottage waiting to have our photographs taken. The people on the island are as real as anywhere else, and we've got the same problems. What we need is a Government who'll do less kowtowing to the wealthy come-overs and do a bit more to convince the young folk that there's some sort of future for them on the island.'

They both thought that the only way to bring lasting prosperity was to make the island a duty-free state, and it was an idea I was to hear put forward time and again throughout my tour.

I mentioned the wreck below Jurby Head and was overjoyed to find that the older of the two remembered its going aground in a gale in the 1920s.

'1929 I think it was,' he said, scratching his head thoughtfully. 'She was a little cargo boat that used to trade between Northern Ireland and Peel, and when I was a lad

I often saw her going up and down the coast. I can't quite remember her name, but I think it was the *Pattaduiee* or something like that. She developed engine trouble and drifted onto the Head. I watched them haul her cargo, and as many bits of her as they could unscrew, up the cliffs with a traction engine. Then they just left her. I wouldn't be surprised if there's a photograph or two of her about somewhere. There might even be some information in the Manx Museum in Douglas.'

In the Manx language the word 'Cronk' means a hill, but when I waved goodbye to the friendly council men and set off through the village of The Cronk, there was little more than a slight undulation in the road to indicate we had reached a summit. From The Cronk to Ballaugh, where I would have liked to visit what is reputed to be the oldest church on the island, was two miles by main road, but a minor road leading to Orrisdale looked more attractive on the map and I led Thor along it. The sun had warmed the air, and it was blissfully peaceful, with only the clip-clop of Thor's iron shoes on the tarmac breaking the stillness.

In the distance the ridges of Slieau Curn and Slieau Freoaghane looked superb against a background of blue sky, and I stopped to take photographs. While I was busy, Thor decided to do a little exploring on his own account and turned off down a lane leading to a disused sand quarry. It was an ideal place to stop for a bite of lunch, so I relieved him of the packs and, while he grazed and dozed, I assembled the stove and made a delicious soup with the help of packets of dehydrated vegetables and dried meat. One of the delicacies given me to try by a manufacturer was German rye bread which I can only liken to chewing slabs of felt underlay. No doubt it is highly nutritious, and presumably someone must eat it or manufacturers would not make it, but it rates a zero in my top ten favourite foods.

Thor showed no reluctance to leave the grass, and it was a sure sign that he was thirsty. Usually if I cannot find water for him I make a hollow in the ground, line it with a plastic bag, and fill it from a two-gallon container I carry in the packs, but I had used the last drop to make a mug of coffee to kill the taste of the rye bread. The map showed a stream at Bishop's Glen, about a mile and a half away on the road to Kirk Michael, and we set off at a cracking pace as if Thor could smell the water. And for a change he led me!

The full title of the Anglican Bishop of the Isle of Man is the Bishop of Sodor and Man, though why it should be, no one is quite sure. Some historians say that it goes back to the time when the Vikings ruled Scotland and the Isle of Man. They called the Hebrides and the Western Isles of Scotland 'Sodor' to distinguish the region from their more southerly kingdom of Man. Even though ties with the Viking empire were severed in the thirteenth century, and the last connection with Scotland in the fourteenth century, the Manx Bishops retained the title of 'Sodor and Man' and were given a rather nice house to go with it.

Bishop's Court, a large, rambling building with its own private chapel, lies about half way between Ballaugh and Kirk Michael at the foot of Bishop's Glen, and with a history going back to the twelfth century successive gardeners have left a legacy of superbly laid out tree-lined gardens which, especially when the rhododendrons are in bloom, are a mass of colour. The bishops took the care of the garden very seriously, and in 1677 Bishop Bridgman even went to the extent of drawing up a contract of employment between himself and his gardener, in which 'David Anderson Scotchman ... professeth and taketh upon him to have served persons of quality in the respective conditions of a Gardiner Cook Caterar Groome Baker and Brewer ... now offerath his service unto the Sd.Bp ... and more particularly in and about his Gardens which hee shall cultivate workmanlike and by digging planting sowing keeping neat and safe shall improve to the best advantage in rearing a seminary of all manner of fruits hearbs flowers seeds roots and other trees both for profit and pleasure which the soile and clyme of Bopscourt in the Isle of Mann is capable off.'

When David Anderson, Scotchman, was employed at Bishop's Court, the sight of a pony being led into the gardens would not have aroused much attention, but when I tramped up the drive leading Thor, the resident gardener stood open-mouthed with horror, as if he had seen a ghost. It was when the ghost asked if he could get a bucket of water for his thirsty pony that the gardener realized we were real, and though in normal circumstances he was probably a friendly and hospitable chap, the vision of a line of hoofprints across his beloved lawns was too much – he told me to get the blazes out of the garden and into the glen, where there was a stream.

In days gone by, apart from having a nice house, the incumbent bishop also had a private glen, where by means of a gently meandering path he could take advantage of climbing a couple of hundred feet nearer to the heavens when, like Moses on Mount Sinai, he was summoned to a private consultation with the Almighty. Away from the pristine formality of the gardens around the house, the bishops' gardeners of a century ago planted a lot of oak, beech, sycamore, birch, larch and Scots pine in the glen. In the course of time nature carpeted the gaps between the trees with brilliant flowers, slender ferns, mosses, wild garlic, ivy and all manner of shrubs. The warming effect of the Gulf Stream swirling around the island encourages the growth of palm trees and, though at first it is rather startling to discover them sprouting among the conventional European trees, the old gardeners have planted them to great effect along the footpaths.

To Thor the glen offered the two ingredients dear to his stomach, a plentiful supply of water and grass, and leaving him to gorge himself on both I followed a well-worn footpath and climbed to a small cave cut into the side of a rock. Above the cave someone had chiselled an inscription, 'Lead me to the rock that is higher than I', and inside there was a ledge, well back, so that for anyone sitting on it there could be no distractions from the world outside. It was the perfect place for quiet meditation, and I thought about the bishops who, on many occasions throughout the island's turbulent history, must have withdrawn into its darkness to seek guidance.

Perhaps the most notable of all the early Bishops of

Sodor and Man was Bishop Wilson, who was appointed in 1698 when he was thirty-five. The son of a Cheshire farmer and educated at Trinity College, Dublin, he had the advantage of being an academic who understood the problems of the rustic and was often out of favour with officialdom for defending the rights of the poor. In keeping with an era when the people were very much under the thumb of the Church, he preached an uncompromising 'hell-fire and brimstone' brand of salvation.

It is an odd paradox that a man who is said to have given half his salary to charity and supported hundreds of families during a period of famine on the island should zealously enforce Church discipline to the point of barbarity. A man compelled to stand inside the church door for three Sundays for not being nice to his mother-in-law might be considered reasonable enough, or being clapped in the stocks for a day for taking the Lord's name in vain, but nailing someone by the ears to a pillory for performing a marriage when forbidden to do so seems a rather harsh way of making a chap listen to reason.

People beat a path to the Bishop's door with the strangest petitions: 'The Devil take Billy Wattleworth for having such bad ale' was enough to have poor Billy's pub closed down, and a complaint from a young woman that her boyfriend had got 'the clap, or foul disease' must have put the brake on his amorous activities for months when the information was disclosed from the pulpit. Another quaint law of the Church was that if a man called a woman a bitch, or the woman called the man a dog, or either hurled any other form of abuse, then, 'The person convicted shall be made to stand in the Market Place on a scaffold with their tongue in a noose of leather, and having been thus exposed to the view of the people for some time they are obliged to say three times "Tongue, thou hast lied."'

If the good Bishop was alive today, he would have a field day if he sat through the proceedings in the House of Commons. He might also have recommended that an eighteenth-century punishment meted out to a man convicted of a sexual attack on a woman might be equally effective in today's society. The judge would hand the woman a rope, a sword and a ring and she could choose to have the man hanged or beheaded or to marry him.

It was women who suffered the severest punishments for transgressing the laws of the Church, particularly those relating to sexual morality, and on one occasion the holy Bishop went beyond the bounds of reason in his determination to 'cleanse the soul' of the unfortunate Kathrine Kinred: 'Forasmuch as neither Christian advice or gentle methods of punishments are found to have any effect on Kathrine Kinred, who has brought forth illegitimate children and still continues to strowl about the country, and to lead a most vicious and scandalous life ... [she] is hereby ordered to be dragged after a boat in the sea at Peeltown at the height of the market ... and the constable and souldiers of ye garrison are, by the Governor's order, to be aiding and assisting in seeing this censure performed.'

Appalled by the brutality of the Bishop's order, the boatmen at first refused but, threatened with heavy fines for contempt of court, they were forced to carry it out.

Despite his relentless persecution of 'evildoers', the Bishop was extraordinarily popular, and for over fifty-seven years he travelled on horseback in all weathers to preach throughout the island. A fluent Manx-speaker and scholar, he published several books in the Manx language, and it was through his efforts that the Manx Act of Settlement was passed in 1704 which gave people security of tenure in their houses. He was ninety-three when he died, and his life is a fascinating chapter in the history of the island.

I left the cave feeling cold and stiff but outside the air was warm, and a brisk walk up the tree-lined glen soon had the blood flowing again.

Near the head of the glen was a large ornamental pond overhung with trees and shrubs and alive with small fish leaping high to snatch at the clouds of flies hovering above the water. The activity of the fish had attracted a heron, and he stood motionless on a fallen branch at the water's edge, his long beak poised ready to strike. It was a lovely sight and I crawled stealthily through the undergrowth to photograph him. When a twig snapped under my weight, he looked up in alarm and I held my breath while he stared in my direction, wings spread ready for instant take-off. A fish leapt out of the water almost at his feet and he grabbed it, swallowed it and took up his stance again, eager for the next one.

I breathed a sigh of relief and crept slowly nearer to the pond. Resting the camera on a mound of grass, I focused carefully and was about to press the shutter release when the heron leapt into the air and flew off over the pond with a loud squawk. I froze, hoping he would land again, but he had seen movement on the path and flapped out of sight over the trees. A woman appeared, walking slowly along the edge of the pool, and before I could climb out of my hiding-place, she sank back against the trunk of a tree, only yards from where I was lying, and burst into tears. To witness the grief and tears of someone you know is distressing enough, but to be hidden almost within touching distance of a perfect stranger while her body is convulsed with anguish and uncontrollable sobbing is truly heart-rending. Hardly daring to breathe in case I was discovered, I lay perfectly still, conscious of the many times the women in my own life may have suffered the same misery.

Half an hour passed before she stopped crying, and I was beginning to get the most agonizing cramp in my legs. She wiped her eyes with a paper tissue and got to her feet. At first I thought she was about to go back down the path, but she turned, walked towards the pond to throw the tissue in the water and saw me. She stared down for what seemed a long time, and her mouth opened as if she was going to scream, but she said quietly: 'Have you been watching me?'

I nodded and said: 'Yes, but I didn't mean to! I was trying to photograph a heron, and you were so upset I didn't want to disturb you.' The words sounded hollow and unconvincing.

'It was good of you to be so considerate,' she said. There was no expression in her voice, but I had the feeling she meant it.

I scrambled out from under my bush and, not knowing what to say, fiddled with my cameras, unscrewing lenses, polishing them with the sleeve of my shirt and screwing them back on again. She sank down and rested against the tree wearily.

'Is that your pony by the gate into the glen?' she asked.

I said it was, and hoped he was behaving himself and not eating all the flowers. A flicker of a smile crossed her face.

'He's nice! I had a pony like him when I was a girl.' She pulled a field daisy out of the grass and slowly plucked the petals off it. 'If only those lovely times would come back again,' she murmured, and tears trickled down her cheeks and dropped into the grass. She brushed them angrily away with the back of her hand and dug into her coat pocket for a tissue. 'I'm so sorry,' she sniffed. 'It must be fearfully embarrassing for you. Do please forgive me. I'm not always like this, I promise.'

'It's all right,' I said gently. 'I'm sorry I intruded. I honestly didn't mean to.' I slung my camera bag over my shoulder and turned to walk away.

'Please don't go,' she said quickly. 'It's such a peaceful glen, and I really don't want to drive you away. Perhaps the heron will come back.'

I sensed she was desperate to talk to someone.

'Well, it's worth a try,' I said. 'With all the fish jumping, he might come back.'

I knew there was little chance of the heron returning, but I fixed the camera on a small tripod by the edge of the pond and sat on a tree stump. For a while neither of us spoke, and the only sounds were the plopping of the fish jumping in the pond and the cooing of a wood pigeon hidden in the trees. The woman fumbled in her pocket, produced a packet of cigarettes and lit one.

'Where are you from?' she asked.

I told her about my home in the Lake District, and about the journeys I made with Thor and Lucy.

'I envy you,' she said wistfully. 'Being a writer free to

wander anywhere sounds idyllic.'

'Well, it's certainly more attractive than working in a factory, I grant you,' I laughed, 'but it has its disadvantages too. You might find it hard to believe, but the man who sweeps the streets in my local village earns twice as much as I do.'

The woman shrugged her shoulders. 'It all depends what you want out of life. Money isn't everything. It can provide you with all the material things in life, but that's all! I have everything I could ever need, but I'm married to an arrogant, conceited bully, whose only interest in life is making money, and I'm simply a plaything to pass the time with between deals, or to look decorative when he invites his money-grabbing friends to dinner.

'But it's a horribly artificial way of life, and it's driving me crazy. I've pleaded with him to let us live quietly on the island, and go for lots of walks and enjoy the countryside, but he only jeers at me and says that's for wallies.'

She was close to tears again, and I looked at my watch and said I ought to be getting back to Thor. We walked down the glen together and found Thor taking an afternoon nap in the shade of a large rhododendron bush.

'God, I bet I look a mess!' the woman exclaimed, tugging at her hair. 'Do you happen to have a comb?'

Taking my toilet bag and a towel out of one of the packs, I handed them to her. Washing her face in the stream and combing her hair cheered her up, and she chattered about birds and wild flowers she had seen on the island.

'You really must visit Calf Island while you're here,' she insisted. 'It simply teems with bird life. It's heaven.'

I loaded the packs onto Thor, and we were ready to move on. The woman gripped my hand.

'I'm truly glad I met you, and I hope you have a super journey. My husband doesn't know what he's missing in life.'

'Well, I suppose we all have different priorities,' I said. 'I must admit it would be nice to have money, though I'd use it in a different way from your husband. Money buys time, time to explore with my ponies and write about the journeys without being hounded by bank managers and worrying about the stack of bills mounting up while·I'm away, and how I'm going to pay for a load of hay to feed the ponies in the winter. That's how I'd use money!'

Her face broke into a wide smile, and I was uncomfortably aware of how beautiful she was. She squeezed my hand again.

'It's a nice thought,' she said softly, 'but don't waste your time approaching business tycoons for help. They wouldn't understand what you were talking about; there isn't an atom of humanity in them.'

She moved closer, and for one exciting moment I thought she was going to put her arms round me, but she brushed past, planted a big kiss on Thor's forehead and with a wave walked off through the trees.

'You lucky devil!' I said enviously to Thor as I led him out of Bishop's Glen. 'What's so attractive about you that makes women want to kiss you?'

7

Donald's Bell
and Manannan's Chair

When Frank Keig, Chairman of the Isle of Man Light Horse Society, met me off the boat in Douglas, he had insisted that when I reached Kirk Michael I should stay at his house and had given me precise instructions how to get there.

Kirk Michael was only two miles from Bishop's Court, but to avoid the drudgery of the main road I walked back towards Ballaugh for half a mile or so to join an overgrown track which in the unhurried days of steam locomotives had been the line of the Manx Northern Railway, running from Ramsey to St John's via Ballaugh and Kirk Michael. It must have been a delightful journey as the train chuffed west from Ramsey, following the Sulby river round the foot of the northern hills through the Curraghs to Ballaugh before curving south to Kirk Michael and along the cliff top almost to Peel, where it turned inland to connect at St John's with a line to Douglas operated by another company.

Like many railways elsewhere in the UK, it ground to a halt because not enough people used it. Had the island fathers been blessed with a little more foresight at the time the railway companies folded, they might have realized they had a ready-made tourist attraction. For relatively little outlay, the courses of the railways could have been declared scenic ways for the use of walkers, cyclists and horse-riders. Some of the station buildings along the routes might even have been used as inexpensive overnight accommodation.

Only a stray dog witnessed the historic occasion at a level crossing near Orrisdale when Thor pioneered the first phase of the great Isle of Man scenic route, and I unwound yards of rusty wire and chain to drag the gate sideways and declare the route officially open. In grassy areas where nature is left to its own devices, the result is often a proliferation of wild flowers, and on both sides of the railway track there were masses of Ox-eye Daisies, Herb Robert, Pink Campion, Yellow Ragwort and fern. Thor enjoyed the walk for the amount of food he could snatch, though by the time we reached the outskirts of Kirk Michael the fermenting action of a combination of lush grass and wild garlic rumbled in his stomach like distant thunder, and had it not been for an offshore wind, the lethal gasses erupting from his rear end would have wiped out the whole village!

We negotiated two more sets of level-crossing gates without much difficulty, but Thor took one look at a rusty metal bridge spanning an embankment and refused to budge. Perhaps he remembered Lucy's accident during our journey round Scotland (*Saddle Tramp in the Highlands*), but whatever it was, he made it clear he was not prepared to risk as much as a hoof on the bridge, and that was that! Even when I wafted a Mars bar under his nose there was not the merest ripple of interest, and the crackle of paper around Polo mints had no effect either. Irritated by his obstinacy, I purposefully sat on the ground in front of him and ate them myself.

'Do you need any help?' asked a voice, and I turned to find an old man grinning at me from the other side of the bridge. 'If I get behind him, maybe between us we'll get him across.'

While I stood on the bridge and heaved on the lead rope, the old man walked slowly up behind Thor, took a deep breath and let out an ear-splitting yell that echoed across the fields. The effect was instant! With one bound Thor cleared the bridge and ran for his life along the track. The old man puffed on his pipe and looked very pleased with himself.

'Used to keep hosses myself,' he chuckled. 'Never let 'em

be boss, I say. Don't worry, he'll not get far – there's a gate across the old station yard.'

We leant across the bridge parapet and chatted for a while, and he almost choked with laughter when I told him about my encounter with the gardener at Bishop's Court.

'By God,' he chortled. 'I bet that gave him a fright. He's quite a nice feller really, but he has to be on his toes now that the gardens are private.'

'Private?' I echoed. 'I thought the Bishop lived there.'

'Not any more, he don't! It hasn't been the Bishop's house for many a year. He's got a smart house in Douglas now. Apparently one of them said it was too big and cold to live in, or maybe his missus did.' It was obviously a sore point with the old man, and he banged his pipe angrily on the metal parapet. 'It's a damn disgrace that someone should be allowed to bring hundreds of years of tradition to an end just because they didn't fancy living in the house.' The veins on the old man's forehead were almost at bursting point and, fearing for his blood pressure, I hastily changed the subject by asking if he could direct me to Frank Keig's house.

'Get thee 'oss and follow me,' he replied gruffly.

The Keig family are mad about horses and gave Thor full VIP treatment with lashings of food, a huge loose-box with fresh straw, and more grooming and hoof-polishing than he had enjoyed in months.

'But where's your other pony?' asked Frank.

'She went lame on me near the Point of Ayre,' I said, and went on to explain how I had been forced to leave her behind at Grenaby Farm.

'I know John Huyton well!' exclaimed Frank. 'I'll ring him to find out what the latest is.'

Frank's wife Nancy had laid on a huge tea for me, and while he went into his study to phone, I was ushered to the kitchen table and ordered to tuck in. (The Keigs also refused to let me pitch my tent, and that night I slept in a luxurious bedroom, feeling guilty but ecstatic.)

'John says she's stopped limping,' said Frank cheerfully when he returned to the kitchen, 'but the vet advises resting her for a few more days to be on the safe side.'

I was overjoyed at the news. Leaving Lucy behind had

been a great wrench, and it had rather taken the edge off the enjoyment of the journey.

After the meal Frank drove me down to the village, first to meet his father, who was a gifted wood-carver, then to show me some of his work – an incredibly beautiful pulpit in the local church; finally to the village pub for a glass of beer and a yarn with the locals.

During a heated discussion about the weather, one of the locals in the pub said he knew there was going to be a hot spell if his wife was waiting at the door, rolling pin in hand, when he arrived home after a night out. When I went out to the paddock early the next morning, there was every sign that the long-suffering wife's rolling pin had been very active. The solitary red orb of the sun was climbing above the rim of the hills into a deep purple sky, and along the coast the sea shone like molten gold. There was not the slightest sound or movement, and it was as if everything on earth was spellbound by the glory of the morning. I sat for a long time watching the landscape change shape as the new day grew stronger, but finally the aroma of bacon wafting from the kitchen drove me inside for breakfast.

Gaynor and Nicola, Frank's daughters, had put so much effort into grooming Thor and polishing the pack saddle and harness that I felt positively shabby standing alongside him. With washed mane and tail and glistening body he looked very handsome, and it reminded me of the many happy times spent preparing him for the annual Fell Pony Show at Penrith in Cumberland, where to everyone's amazement he actually won the Veteran's Cup two years in succession.

The family gathered to see us off and, with a shower of kisses for Thor and handshakes for me, we left the stable yard and set off down the road to Kirk Michael village.

'Don't worry about your other pony,' shouted Frank. 'As soon as she's fit I'll collect her in our horse-box and bring her to wherever you happen to be.'

It was typical of Frank! He was a mine of useful information about the island, and though he had enough problems of his own, struggling to keep the family building business alive during a period of recession, nothing was too much trouble in making my stay on the island an enjoyable one. I was deeply saddened when, some months after I had finished my journey, I learnt that he had died of cancer.

It was only ten o'clock in the morning when I led the way through Kirk Michael onto the coast road to Peel, but already the sun was blisteringly hot. Rivulets of tar ran in the gutters, and at every step Thor's heavy shoes sank into the surface of the road like branding-irons. If later the Manx Government's road surveyor had followed the tell-tale hoofprints, he would have noted with relief that the damage to his sacred tarmac ceased about a mile and a half outside the village, when the offending animal turned left into Glen Mooar.

'You must go through Glen Mooar,' Frank Keig had insisted. 'The girls and I rode through it early this year. It's a drove road. You'll love it.'

Compared with some of the mighty glens of the Scottish Highlands, the Manx versions are barely more than dents in the hillsides, but what they lack in grandeur is more than compensated for in their picturesque beauty. Glen Mooar is not a glen to stir the grandiloquence of the promoters of Manx tourism, but it does claim to have the highest water-fall on the island, and it has its own tragic little story ...

In the old days it was a terrible sin to work on the Sabbath, and yet of all people the biggest culprit was the local minister, and he was warned he would meet a sudden and terrible end.

'Are you not ashamed to be doing work on the Sabbath, and the people waiting at the chapel for you?' scolded his housekeeper one Sunday when she discovered the minister mending his boots.

'What are you talking about, woman?' said the minister. 'Go and count the eggs and see how many are in the nest.' The minister was never sure what day it was, but kept a hen which laid one egg a day and when there were seven in the nest, he knew it was the Sabbath.

'There are seven in the nest,' answered the housekeeper.

Panicking at the thought of being late for his service, the

minister pulled his boots on and ran off down the road, but he had forgotten to tie his laces, and when he was by Spooyt Vane waterfall he tripped, fell into the water and was swept away.

A sad end for the minister, but the moral of the story is not clear. Either it is pointing the way to Exodus, Chapter 20, verse 8, 'Remember the Sabbath day, to keep it holy', or it is simply a warning not to trip over your bootlaces.

Shortly after leaving the main road we passed a field where a group of people were busy laying out jumps and obstacles for a gymkhana, and a convoy of landrovers and trailers was unloading excited youngsters and squealing ponies. Within minutes it was pandemonium, with hot-faced officials, loud-voiced parents and anxious competitors rushing in all directions. How the events ever got started was a miracle, but they did, and by that time we were well away from the noise, following a pleasant track overhung with tall bushes.

Thor was gasping with the heat, and when the track dipped down to a ford we rested while he gulped at the water. Sweat dripping off his body like a leaking radiator had spoiled the debonair, well-groomed appearance, and he looked more like his old self again. Continuing up a steep, rocky path, we climbed above the trees and into the full glare of the sun. The view over Kirk Michael and along the coast to the Point of Ayre was fantastic. For a mile an easy grass track wound between mature meadows and ancient hedgerows, a strong indication that it had been an important route in its time; but above the glen, to provide easy access to the farms along the way, the drove road had been widened and surfaced.

I had tied Thor to a gate and was busy taking photographs when a man driving a rickety van drove by, stamped on the brake, reversed back again and wound his window down.

'Hell, I thought I was seeing things,' he laughed. 'What's the pony carrying?'

I told him about my journey, and that Thor was carrying my food and camping equipment.

'Well, I'll be damned!' he exclaimed. 'I've never seen the

like of it in my life. You'll be ready for a cup of tea. Call at the farm on your way past. You can't miss it. It's the one with the bell tower on the barn. I'll get the missus to put the kettle on.' He rammed the van into gear and it lurched away leaving a pall of blue smoke shimmering in the hot air.

The first farm we reached had no bell tower, but the farmer certainly had a passion for collecting buses. Both sides of the road were lined with ex-Douglas Corporation double-deckers and coaches of all ages. I hesitated for a minute or two: what with one farmer boasting a bell tower on his barn and another littering the countryside with buses, I began to wonder if I had wandered into some strange community, but curiosity got the better of me and I carried on. The exertion of carrying the heavy packs in the fierce heat slowed Thor to a snail's pace, and it was over half an hour before the next farm hove into sight. It was unmistakable! There, built onto one end of the roof of a stone barn adjoining the house, was a belfry, complete with bell.

'I rescued it from Cronk y Voddy church when it was closed,' explained the farmer proudly when I led Thor into the farmyard and stared up at the beautifully built stone belfry. 'Listen to this!' He heaved on a rope hanging down the gable end of the barn, and the deep clang of the bell reverberated round the buildings. 'Lovely sound, isn't it? And to think it might have been lost for ever.' He hung the end of the rope on a nail. 'Come on in and have a bite to eat. By the way, I'm Donald Cannon.'

Leaving Thor dozing in the shade of the byre, I sank gratefully into an armchair in the farm kitchen, and while we worked our way through a mound of sandwiches, scones and cakes and drank mugs of tea, Donald told me that his family had attended Cronk y Voddy church for years, and when he was a lad they never missed a service whatever the weather. The church was only a mile from the farm, but he said that in a winter gale and deep snow it could take hours to get there.

'That bell was as much part of our lives as the farm itself,' said Donald, pointing in the direction of Cronk y

Voddy with his mug of tea, 'and when I heard that the church was to be sold, I nipped in and bought the bell before anyone else could get it.'

His wife topped up our mugs from a large tea-pot. 'Aye,' she said laughingly, 'we heard that the Bishop wanted the bell for East Baldwin. I'd love to know what he said to the minister when he heard we'd got it.'

'Cronk y Voddy's got more right to it than the Bishop!' snorted Donald. 'The bell's on that roof now, and it'll stay there for all time.'

I was reluctant to leave the coolness of the kitchen and return to the relentless heat outside, but I wanted to visit Peel before going on to Foxdale to camp for the night, and it was a long detour. Thanking Donald and his wife for their hospitality, I loaded the packs on Thor and continued on my journey.

'If you're interested in Manx history, stop off at Manannan's Chair,' Donald called as I rode out of the yard. 'Third field on the left. You can't miss it. It's a big green mound.'

The bell clanged a farewell as we tramped down the quiet country road, and as it resounded across the shimmering fields I could well understand Donald's determination to cling to a symbol of an era when the pace of life was less pressured and when people in the community had a sense of belonging.

Manannan Mac Lir – Manannan of the Sea, the legendary first ruler of Man, is one of the most colourful characters in Manx folklore. He lived in a castle on the top of South Barrule, a hill just south of Foxdale, and it is said he had magical powers over the sea – 'From his prescience of the change of the weather [he] always avoided tempests.' Perhaps it was not so much prescience as the good view he had from his castle: he could see storm clouds approaching long before anyone else. But to the Manx fishermen he was a saint, and before putting to sea they prayed for his help and guidance. A forerunner of today's invincible American TV detective hero, he rode a horse called Enbarr which could travel over land and sea, wore an impregnable suit of armour and wielded a sword called 'The Answerer'.

When the first Vikings appeared in Peel Bay, Manannan's magic was really put to the test, but with the aid of a few chips of wood and an incantation or two he produced a large fleet of ships which panicked the invaders into sailing away again. In quieter moments he liked to survey his kingdom from a large mound now known as Manannan's Chair, but it is an odd choice for a vantage point for, unless his magical powers enabled him to see over hills, he could never have enjoyed more than a limited view of the island's west coast. Somewhere along the way, Manannan's magic seems to have lost its potency, and in time the Vikings conquered the island and introduced their own rulers. From that day Manannan bore a grudge against anyone of noble descent, and if they dared to venture onto the island he would envelop it in a thick mist.

When I walked into Peel late that morning, it was obvious to all which side of the social divide I had been born on: it was a clear day and you could see for miles!

In 1836 a visitor to the Isle of Man wrote, 'Since the decay of the herring fishing Peel has gradually declined, and is now of insignificant importance; the curiosity of strangers and a few surrounding families infusing into it what little life remains. A number of idle fellows standing all day with their hands in their pockets, or arms akimbo in the market basking like dogs in the sun.' When I led Thor through the town and onto the quayside, there was little evidence of the slothful living the writer complained of, apart from a couple of fishermen and a few visitors sitting outside a pub enjoying their drinks, but there is no doubt that Peel is only a shadow of its former prominence as the centre of the island's fishing industry.

That Manx judges still promise to execute the laws of the Isle of Man 'as indifferently as the herring backbone doth lie in the middle of the fish' gives some indication of how important the herring-fishing industry was to the island's survival. To the fishermen, the herring was 'King of the Sea', and by smoking it over wood chippings they created the kipper, a delicacy for which the Isle of Man is legendary. There was a time when, even in the furthest outposts of the south of England, if someone was asked what they knew about the Isle of Man, they were almost certain to reply 'kippers'. The humble Manx kipper still graces the tables of all stratas of society, but on nothing like the scale it used to. One reason is changing tastes, but another, and the one that sounded the death knell of the Manx fishing industry in the last century, is that the vast shoals of herring which could once be relied upon to appear as regularly as the seasons just vanished. Over the years they have returned in smaller numbers, but modern fishing techniques, assisted by electronic fish-finding equipment, have resulted in over-fishing and the introduction of quotas in order to save the herring from becoming a museum piece. The decline in fish stocks affected all Manx ports, but Peel suffered most of all.

'The Scotch and Irish boats land in Peel,' a fisherman told me as he mended a net spread out on the quayside, 'but you'll hardly see a Manx boat among 'em. My grandfather used to tell of the time when the harbour was full of local boats, and it's not so long ago when that area along the quay, that's now a car-park and exhibition hall for the Viking boat, was curing sheds employing hundreds of people. Peel's just a ghost town now!' He finished mending the hole and heaved the net onto the deck of his boat. 'I know one thing for certain,' he continued. 'The day's not far away when the Government will have to decide whether it wants a fishing industry on the island or whether we are just another tourist attraction.'

A truck arrived to unload fish boxes, and Thor was in the way, so I walked him down to the car-park and secured him to a railing by the Viking boat shed. I borrowed a plastic bucket off the fisherman and, having filled it at the tap on the quayside, gave Thor a drink. I left him chewing a few pieces of apple and half a packet of Polo mints while I bought a ticket and wandered around the Viking exhibition.

The star of the show was *Odin's Raven*, a fifty-foot

replica of a Viking longship, built in Norway and sailed to the Isle of Man to mark the millennium – the one-thousandth anniversary of Tynwald, the island's Parliament. It was the idea of an island businessman, Robin Bigland, and he was part of the sixteen-man crew of Manxmen and Norwegians who sailed the boat across, arriving just in time for the visit of HM The Queen, who presided for the first time as Lord of Man at the Tynwald celebrations in 1979.

The 1,500-mile journey was covered in true Viking style, with the crew rowing or sailing as the weather dictated, and living on dried reindeer meat, oatcakes, milk, honey and vegetables. On one occasion the boat capsized off the Isle of Skye in heavy seas, but fortunately no one was lost. I was travelling round the West Coast of Scotland with Thor and Lucy during the month of June 1979, and I saw the longboat sailing down the Sound of Mull in torrential rain and squally winds. It was a very courageous voyage, and if those great Viking warriors Magnus Barefoot and Godred Crovan were watching *Odin's Raven* from Valhalla, it must have stirred many exciting memories.

The guide at the exhibition was tall, bearded and dressed in full Viking regalia complete with horned helmet. Not only did he look the part but he was a Viking enthusiast and rolled out the genealogy of the early invaders as if he had known them personally.

'You can't come to Peel without going across to St Patrick's Isle,' he boomed. 'That's where the famous Magnus Barefoot built his castle when he landed on the island in 1098. It was built on a wooden pile – that's how Peel got its name. Then in 1228 King Olaf was wintering his fleet in Peel when Reginald, the son of Godred II – who you may recall was a successor to the great Godred Crovan, ruler of Man and the Hebrides, who reigned 1079–95 and is buried on the Island of Islay in Scotland –' he paused for breath. '– Reginald, who was in exile, raided Peel one night and set fire to all of Olaf's fleet in the harbour. We re-enact it every year. It's a grand sight!'

The guide left me to have his photograph taken with a

party of Japanese visitors, and I returned to the car-park, my head buzzing with the complexities of Viking family squabbles. But the exhibition was no dull museum display. A guide like him brought the place alive, and a school outing to *Odin's Raven* would give the island youngsters more insight into their heritage than a library of history books.

The pedant would insist that St Patrick's Isle lost its island status when, towards the end of the last century, a causeway and an outer harbour were built to provide landing facilities for fishing vessels at all states of the tide, but technicalities could never spoil the enjoyment of wandering around the ruins of the large Viking settlement and the thirteenth-century cathedral. History almost oozes out of the soft turf of this tiny island, which was an important fortified dwelling when most of Britain's teeming cities were dinosaurs' watering holes.

I would have liked to have spent a whole day in Peel but there was no shade to leave Thor under, and the custodian made it quite clear that a pony would not be permitted to graze among the Viking ruins, even if he was called 'Thor'.

The distance from Peel to St John's is about four miles, but it felt a lot longer. I had hoped to follow the course of the old railway but, when I was searching for it, a man told me it was blocked in several places. There was no option but to follow the main road, and it was nerve-racking. The amount of traffic on the island is light compared with the overburdened roads of mainland Britain, but it is not without its crazy drivers, and on the day we were heading for St John's one was attempting to clip a micro-second off the speed record between Peel and Douglas. Driving a ramshackle Ford bristling with aerials, he roared in and out of a line of farm vehicles heading for an auction at St John's and caused chaos among the loads of cattle and sheep when drivers were forced to brake sharply to avoid a collision. The lunatic came within inches of mowing Thor down when he drove along the banking on the wrong side of the road, and if he ever reached Douglas without killing some innocent, I trust that an act of Providence rid the world of a menace by directing him off the end of the pier into the sea!

I was hot and angry when I reached St John's, and sorely in need of a large glass of iced shandy, so I made straight for a pub close to the auction mart. The yard was seething with people and animals, and there was not an inch of space in which to leave Thor. A kindly farmer came to the rescue with the offer of an empty trailer and, accepting gratefully, I unloaded the packs, fetched Thor a bucket of water and pushed through the crowded bar to order a pint of shandy and a meat pie. Having poured the drink, the landlord said that only full meals were served in the lounge bar, and if I wanted a pie I would have to go through to the public bar. I said that surely, since both rooms were served by the same bar and all he had to do was reach behind him and lift a pie from one side of the bar to the other, it would be much easier than my having to fight my way round to the other side of the crowded pub.

'Those are the rules!' he said sourly.

'In that case,' I said, 'I'll find a pub where the rules suit the customer and not the landlord.'

Leaving my drink, I pushed my way back outside and sat in Thor's trailer and fumed.

The auction was in full swing when I walked across to the mart and, as the auctioneer gabbled out a stream of incomprehensible patter, I watched pens of sheep and cattle change hands without anyone around the crowded sale ring as much as raising a finger or twitching an eyebrow. Seasoned auction-goers develop a code of scarcely detectable facial tremors which auctioneers learn to recognize, and farmers are unequalled masters of the art.

Two farmers standing with their backs to the auctioneer were having a fierce argument with a lorry-driver about haulage charges. They could not possibly have seen the sheep brought into the ring, yet, when the bidding was finished, one turned to the other and said, 'You got 'em cheap, John. Put 'em in my wagon and I'll stop off at your place on my way home.'

For all their skill at driving a shrewd bargain, farmers are compulsive buyers who cannot bear to miss a bargain.

When the livestock sales finished, they descended like locusts to bid for rolls of old fencing wire, half-empty tins of paint, rusty scythes, bundles of rakes with broken handles, strange-shaped handtools whose use had been lost in antiquity, boxes of outdated animal medicines and sheep dip, and fiendish looking contraptions for extricating partly born calves and castrating bulls. Most of it was useless junk that would be taken home, dumped in an outhouse and forgotten about until years later, when either the farm was sold or the farmer's son took over and had the whole lot cleared out back to the auction again.

When I returned to Thor, roars of laughter were coming from the back of a wagon parked next to the trailer, where a group of farmers were sitting on the floor eating their lunch.

A short, fat chap in a ragged tweed jacket gulped down the last of his food and said: 'My old dad used to tell a tale about a farmer who lived out Dalby way,' but his mates interrupted with jeers of: 'Thy father was as big a liar as you!'

The story-teller pressed on undaunted.

'No,' he insisted, 'it's a true story but you can believe it or not. Well, this old chap – name of Charlie – was sweet on a widow woman who lived about Port Erin, whose husband had left her a bit of money, and Charlie used to spend a lot of time visiting her. At first she wouldn't have anything to do with him, but eventually she married him and he took her back to the farm. Trouble was, he had a terrible weakness for horses, and with the money the widow brought he was always buying a fresh one, and he'd bring it home and parade it up and down in front of his missus. Anyway, one day he brings this big horse home, and he was that proud of it he shouts for his missus to come out and look at it. She came fleeing down in a right temper, yelling at him to put the damned horse away and get on with some work around the spot. "And I'll tell you something," she shouts. "If it weren't for my money, that horse wouldn't be here!" Old Charlie looks at her and he says: "And I'll tell thee something too. If it wasn't for thy money, thee wouldn't be here either!" '

Odin's Raven arriving to celebrate the Manx parliament's 1000th
birthday

Douglas Harbour – sea gateway to the island

The schooner *Peggy* – discovered in a secret boathouse after 200
years

Laurence Harwood, Adrian del Nevo and the author studying bird migration maps on the Calf of Man

Nicola and Gaynor Keig loading Thor

Silver sand and sailing ships at Port Erin

'Not much shelter here' – a wet day on the Millennium Way

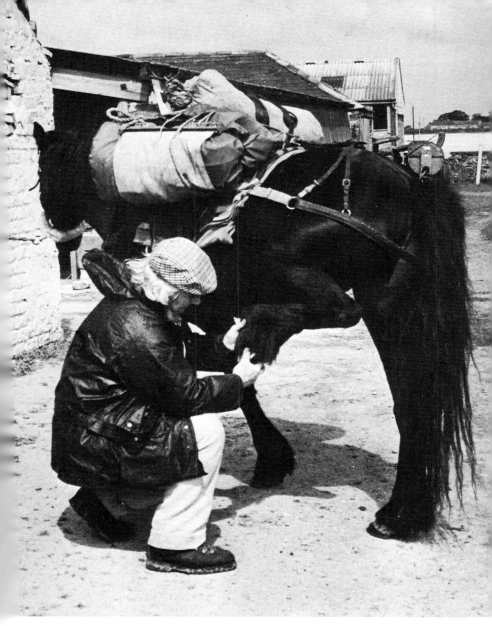

Lucy goes lame

Cushag – a tail-less Manx cat

Thor nervously inspects a World War Two mine on the beach

The 'rescued' Cronk y Voddy church bell finds a new home

The Deemster's Cairn at
East Baldwin

Green hills by the sea – typical Manx countryside

'After you, Thor.' 'No, after you, Lucy.' A stile halts progress below
Snaefell.

The farmers fell about, almost choking on their sandwiches.

'By God, that was a good 'un,' wheezed one of the others, gasping for breath and taking a quick nip from a hip flask. 'But did you ever hear tell of Archie Kermodes, who used to have a lot of sheep running above Sulby Glen years ago?' The others stopped eating to listen.

'He went up to feed 'em one day, and who should be standing at the field gate but the minister. They got talking about farming and one thing and another, and the minister says: "What do you do if only a few of your flock turn up at feeding time?" "Oh, I feeds them," says Archie. "Them 'at turns up gets fed, even if there's only half a dozen." Well, the next Sunday it snowed hard and only a few folk were able to get to the service, but the minister droned on and on with a long sermon, and Archie was getting madder and madder because the weather was turning worse and he wanted to be off home. Anyway, when the service was over, the minister was standing in the church doorway shaking hands when Archie comes out. "Our callings have a lot in common, Archie," says the minister. "Like you, when only a few of my flock turn up, I make sure they are fed." "You certainly do, Minister," shouts Archie, rushing off to get the stock fed before dark, "but when only a few of mine turn up, I don't feed them the whole ruddy bagful!" '

The farmers were having a whale of a time, and laughing with them melted the anger of my brush with the landlord of the pub. Thor was quite content nibbling at a rack of hay in the trailer, and taking my cameras I went to photograph Tynwald Hill and wallow in Manx history.

The popular impression of the early Vikings is of marauding savages who wandered the sea in their longboats, attacking defenceless communities and wallowing in an orgy of bloodshed and fire. This may well have been so, but it was those same savages who introduced a system of legislation into the Isle of Man which has survived for over a thousand years.

The history of the island is long and complex and

requires a lot of explanation. Trying to decide which historian has got it right can be very confusing, but in a nutshell the early Vikings created a system of government called 'Tynwald'. Every year on midsummer's day, the Viking chief stood on a small mound of earth at St John's and read out the laws that had been passed that year, announced any new ones for the approval of the assembly, arbitrated over disputes, said a few prayers to Thor, the god of war, enjoyed a good feast and then settled back to watch the sports (usually rolling convicted criminals down the slopes of Slieau Whallian in spiked barrels).

From the early Viking Tynwald has evolved the Manx Tynwald Court – a sort of combination of the British House of Lords and House of Commons. The upper chamber is the Legislative Council, consisting of eight members elected from the House of Keys, together with the Attorney General and the Bishop of Sodor and Man. Presiding over the Tynwald Court is the Lieutenant-Governor representing the Queen, who holds the title of 'Lord of Man'. The House of Keys has a role similar to that of the House of Commons, though it has only twenty-four elected members presided over by a Speaker who, unlike his counterpart in Westminster, is allowed a vote. Most of the members claim to be independent of any party political system.

Some Manx politicians like to point out that their womenfolk were given the vote long before women on the mainland, but they stop short of explaining that it might have had something to do with the fact that Emily Pankhurst's mother was a Manxwoman.

Every year on 5 July the twenty-four members of the Keys, together with the Lieutenant-Governor, the Bishop, the Attorney General and his two Deemsters (judges) and other dignitaries, assemble with much pomp and ceremony on Tynwald Hill to read the laws in true Viking tradition. Nowadays the dignitaries drive to St John's in a convoy of glittering motor cars, but the cavalcade would look more spectacular if, as in 1794, the Lieutenant-Governor, '... was attended by the Cavalry of the Isle, which consists of a certain number of horsemen, amounting in all to upwards of a hundred. They were properly accoutred, and appeared a remarkably fine-looking body of men.'

Like most basic systems, the Viking administration would have continued to work for the good of everyone on the island, but successive rulers manipulated the laws to their own advantage by appointing their friends and favourites to the House of Keys. It became not so much a Parliament as a rich man's club, which did not care a hoot about the plight of ordinary people. The position was not helped when in 1765 the Duke of Atholl sold the island to the British Government and, 'The colours with the arms of the island were then struck, and the English colours hoisted in their room, and a discharge of three volleys from the troops that were brought over from England.' The British monarch became Lord of Man, and ruled the island with gunboat diplomacy, milking it of what he could and putting nothing back. The House of Keys lost its ancient right to make or amend the laws of the island, and for four years no Tynwald ceremony was held at St John's. It was a black era for the islanders, and it was not until 1866 that the Manx Parliament was given control over its own revenue, on condition that free elections should be allowed; since then the island has been given more and more say in its own destiny.

The Manx Tynwald is the oldest legislative body in Europe, and with low income tax and other perks, the island has a degree of autonomy which is the envy of all who feel strongly that there would be more icing on the cake in their own corner of Britain were it not shackled to a Parliament in London.

Having photographed the tiered mound of Tynwald Hill from every angle, and followed in the footsteps of the mighty to the top, I was on my way to buy Thor an ice-cream when my farmer friend emerged from a hotel nearby and asked if I would take the pony out of the trailer as he wanted to load a cow in it. I thanked him for his hospitality and helped him to load the cow. Then, with Thor licking the remains of a choc-ice off his nose, we set off along the road to Foxdale.

8

Tail-less Cats and a Happy Reunion

The article about me in the Manx newspaper had prompted Judy Corrin, who lives on a smallholding above Foxdale, to write offering help with grazing, and she had sent me a sketch map showing me how to reach it. The quickest way was to stay on the main road, but there was a lot of traffic leaving the auction and I turned off up a minor road to Ballaoates.

For the first half mile or so it climbed steeply up a hill, and both Thor and I were dripping with sweat before the angle eased and we stopped for a rest in the gardens of an abandoned croft house with boarded-up windows and a dilapidated iron roof. Thor enjoyed himself foraging around in overgrown grass until I realized it was yellow ragwort and had to bundle him hurriedly out onto the road. In Manx it is called '*cushag*' and is supposed to cure infections, but it is strange that the islanders should adopt as their national flower one that is highly poisonous to animals.

A farmer driving a Landrover came by and stopped to look at Thor and ask where I was making for. We talked for a while about the way agriculture had changed on the island, and the way the crofting system of a few acres of land with two or three cows and a few sheep could no longer survive.

'We call them "tholtons",' he said, 'and you'll see them all over the island. That was the old way of life, but like so many other things they were a victim of changing times.

The tholtons that were in a reasonable condition have been snapped up as holiday homes, much the same as the crofts in the west of Scotland.

'Was this house a croft?' I asked, pointing to the old house. A broad grin spread over his face.

'Well it might have been in its day,' he laughed, 'but the old folk tell a story about the time when the manager of the Archallagan Mine lived there, before the mine was shut down. His wife couldn't keep off the gin, and as soon as the man went off to work, she'd be away down to Foxdale for another bottle. To get her off the drink he took to locking her in the house every morning before he went to work, but unbeknown to him the wife had a fancy-man who used to creep up to the house and feed her a good shot of gin through the keyhole with a straw.' He laughed and climbed into the Landrover and started the engine. 'It's amazing what some folk will do for a drink. God knows what the fancy-man got out of it though. Courting through a keyhole must be hellish frustrating!' He waved and drove away. 'Have a good journey,' he called. 'One day I'd like to explore the island myself!'

To reach the Corrins' smallholding we had to drop down into Foxdale village, then climb steeply out of it again up the well-named Stoney Mountain Road, but it was worth it. Like so many Manx people, Judy and her husband Peter have a warmth of friendship which, within a short time of meeting them, makes complete strangers feel they have known them all their lives. Judy is a horse fanatic, which meant that Thor had to be fed, watered and fussed over before she would turn her attention to Peter and me, but it gave us the opportunity to relax in the cosy sitting-room of the cottage with a mug of coffee and swap stories about life at sea.

Peter is the captain of one of the Isle of Man Steam Packet Company's ships, and he has been at sea since he left school. He had some fascinating yarns to tell about his early years working on small cargo boats between the Isle of Man and the dozens of small harbours along the Lancashire, Cumberland and Irish coasts, carrying 'everything from coal to cornflakes', but he was deeply concerned about the way the British merchant fleet had declined almost to extinction.

'When the Steam Packet used to berth in Liverpool, watching the ships leaving the Mersey at the top of the tide was like the start of the Monte Carlo rally,' he quipped, 'but these days people stop their cars and stare if they see a ship in the river.'

I asked him what he thought about the suggestion that the Isle of Man should become a Duty Free island similar to the Channel Islands.

'Oh, you've picked a sore subject there,' he replied. 'Some are for it and some are against it. On the face of it there are bound to be more jobs for customs and immigration people, and hopefully better trade for the Steam Packet and the hotels and shops, but although there's been a lot of talk, nobody has really gone into it and spelt out the advantages and disadvantages. I'd certainly like to see an increase in the numbers of visitors to the island – we are really feeling the effect of cheap holidays in the Mediterranean, but I'd like to think that people were coming for something more than cut-price fags and booze.'

I spent an extremely pleasant evening drinking and talking with the Corrins, but it had been a long day and by ten o'clock I was wilting rapidly. Once again the tent remained in its bag while I weakened and accepted the offer of a bed. On a bookshelf in the bedroom was a history of the Isle of Man Steam Packet Company, and before I dropped off to sleep I read it from cover to cover.

I slept so soundly that, had it not been for one of Judy's goats, I might have stayed in bed until midday. It was in the garden munching the roses, and Judy was standing beneath my bedroom window letting fly with a torrent of most un-ladylike words that had the goat fleeing for its life. I made a mental note to try one or two of them on Thor the next time he refused to cross a bridge or wade through a stream.

It was another gorgeously warm, sunny morning, and the hens and ducks were stretched out in the grass making the most of it. Judy was busy milking the goats, and I watched the warm liquid froth into the bucket as she skilfully reduced the swollen udder to a limp bag.

With the popularity of self-sufficiency and an awareness of the value of alternative medicine, the much-maligned goat has been taken more seriously in recent years but, though I've tried rearing them myself, they are creatures I cannot get on with at any price. The brutes would stand perfectly still while my daughters milked them, but as soon as I touched them, there would be milk, goats, buckets and me flying in all directions. They would let anyone fondle their ears and tickle their chins, but when I tried to make friends with one, it would butt me up the backside and send me sprawling into the muckheaps. Let them off their tethers for a second, and they would be away like a flash, chewing every treasured flower and tree to shreds. I became so exasperated with them that I got rid of the lot, vowing that if, in the future, I ever had a grudge against anyone, the surest way to get my revenge would be to buy them a goat!

The most intriguing of all the Corrins' many domestic pets was a little tail-less Manx tabby cat called 'Cushag'. Why Manx cats should be minus the appendage other cats find indispensable as a scarf when sleeping or for waving about when angry, has mystified scientists and academics for decades. A traveller on the island in 1836 noted that, 'The most singular feature in the natural history of this country is that the genuine aboriginal orthodox cats have no tails.' A year later a Mr Bell, in his *History of British Quadrupeds*, was convinced that he had solved the problem of the tail-less cat. He had seen it in a Dorsetshire village, '... where it was rather numerous ... and it was traditional that they had been derived from one which had lost its tail by accident. This opinion is much confirmed by a fact recorded in *London's Magazine* of a cat to which such an accident occurred, and which always had two or three tail-less kittens in every subsequent litter.'

But the scientists were having none of this frivolous speculation: 'A Manx cat may appear to be tail-less,' thundered Miss E.C. Herdman MSc to a meeting of the Isle of Man Natural History and Antiquarian Society in 1930, 'but there are always some caudal vertebrae behind the sacrum ... The deformity may occur at different stages in development. Thus sometimes the cartilaginous vertebrae are abnormal, while in other cases the deformity is due to incomplete ossification.'

The scientific theory might have been accepted, if only because few could understand it, were it not for the Manx poet T.E. Brown, who, in a letter to a little girl, gave the real reason why the Manx cat has no tail: 'When the giant Hercules was wandering round the Isle of Man, he was attacked in Glen Roy near Laxey by an enormous cat, which wrapped its tail round him. After a fierce struggle, Hercules drew his sword and cut off the cat's tail. As a result all its descendants were born without tails.'

Waving goodbye to Judy and Peter, I led a reluctant Thor away from the comforts of the smallholding and followed a quiet lane to the edge of a small forest. At least, it looked small on the map, but after several unsuccessful attempts at finding a way through it, I felt I had wandered into the impregnable fortress of a Foxdale goblin the Corrins had forgotten to warn me about. Having spent an hour tramping up a forest road only to find that it ended abruptly in an abandoned quarry, I studied the map closely and was ashamed to discover that I had been heading in entirely the wrong direction. Poor Thor was plastered in sweat and the dust kicked up off the sandy track, and he had walked for miles carrying the heavy packs in the hot sun only to arrive back at the edge of the forest where we had started from. If ponies could speak, I have a feeling that the normally placid Thor would have told me precisely what he thought of stupid humans.

The path we should have been on was the route of an old drove road, and after searching around I found it hidden in a clump of prickly gorse. It was rough and stony for a while but gradually gave way to soft grass and wild flowers. The aroma of peat and spruce trees hung in the air, and birds sang from every bush. It was one of those mornings when every living creature seemed to be saying how wonderful it was to be alive. Across the valley the brown dome of South Barrule dominated the horizon, a tantalizing invitation to explore beyond, and I strode ahead, eager to see more of this unparalleled island.

Frank Keig had arranged for me to stay with his friends the Watersons who farm at Dalby on the west coast, but though I pored over the map hoping to find a track across the hills, there was none. Leaving the pleasant grassy track there was no alternative but to follow the main Foxdale to Port Erin road as it snaked through a plantation of conifers round South Barrule. I had resigned myself to the usual deadly dull plod up the ribbon of tarmac when, to my joy, high above Foxdale the tree line ended, unfolding a view across Foxdale to the northern hills and through a steep wooded valley to St John's. The Corrins' house stood out as a white speck on a green hillside, and in the distance the sun picked out the rusted iron roof where the mine manager had locked up his gin-loving wife. It was the perfect excuse to laze for a while, and I sat on a rock trying to identify the hills from the map.

Thor always appreciates a good view when we are on a journey, but for a reason different from mine. He knows that a good view means I will spend a lot of time taking photographs or staring into space. It gives him a chance to slink away and sample the local grass and heather or, if no one is about, the prize flowers in the garden of a roadside cottage. Now, taking advantage of my preoccupation with the map, he set off on one of his solo jaunts, and when I looked up he was a black dot heading for a tuft of grass growing beside a derelict building. He had devoured the grass and was about to push his head through a fenced enclosure to snatch at a few plants growing round the edge of a hole when I ran up and heaved him backwards by the tail. Had he but known it, he was standing on the brink of an old mine shaft.

The shaft and a few gaunt skeletons of buildings are all that is left of an industry that at one time brought great prosperity to the little village of Foxdale and, like so many great events in history, it all happened because of a horse – or, to be strictly accurate, it happened because at the time the horse was pulling a cart-load of hay. The weight of the hay pushed the cart wheels deep into the soft ground, and hey presto, out squirted top-quality lead ore! The farmer's dream of owning a boarding house in Douglas could come true – he had hit the jackpot. He probably flung his cap and gaiters in the air and rushed away to buy a pick and shovel, hoping a notice issued in the eighteenth century was still valid. The notice stated that, 'Any person who shall find out any veins of Lead or Copper ... such as shall be thought fitt for working by the Steward or overseer of the said workes ... shall not only have paid down to them fourty shillings as a reward, but shall have the preference of working the said mines ... and three pounds a ton for every ton they shall get ... provided they begin and prosecute the land work within three months.'

The Foxdale lead mines are reputed to have been the richest in Britain, and at the height of production there were over twenty-five miles of underground workings. Both owners and workers prospered as mines opened and the industry grew. The only fly in the ointment as far as the islanders were concerned was the British Government, which, after acquiring the island and its mineral rights from the Duke of Atholl, spirited away enormous royalties into the Treasury. Like all speculative bubbles, the Foxdale mining boom eventually expanded beyond its limits, and it burst in 1912, leaving behind only memories, faded photographs and crumbling buildings. In 1949 the Manx Government gained control of mineral rights on the island, but it was too late. Working the mines was no longer an economic proposition. Unless by some miracle there is a mighty increase in world demand for lead, the abandoned mine workings scattered about the Manx hillsides will remain silent and neglected, tombstones in a forgotten graveyard.

Having been deprived of a meal and suffered the indignity of being hauled backwards by his tail, Thor stood sulking, nose pressed against the wall of one of the ruins, but the sound of a wrapper being torn off a bar of chocolate was too tempting to resist and he trotted over, anxious not to be left out.

Leaving the mine and the main road, we followed a minor road, dropping steeply into a narrow valley bottom before climbing up again to a forest plantation at Arrasy.

According to the map, the road petered out into an unsurfaced track after half a mile, and I was puzzled to find it had been newly surfaced with tarmac and chippings. It seemed an extravagance to spend money upgrading a track that led only to a forest and a remote farm. But when the road reached the top of the hill, I saw the reason: a new Ministry of Defence radio station, bristling with aerials and surrounded by a high wire fencce with a guard on the gate. A van left the compound and drove slowly by, with two men in the front eyeing us suspiciously.

'What's this place?' I called cheerfully to the driver, but he stared at me unsmilingly.

'None of your business,' he replied brusquely. 'Just keep moving!'

The man in the van continued to watch every move as though convinced that at any moment I would put a match to Thor's tail and launch him like a missile at the radio station, but they faded out of sight as we descended slowly to a solitary farmhouse at Garey.

In the days when ponies were the only means of transport on the island, Garey was the junction of four important tracks across the hills, one contouring round the side of Slieau Whallian to St John's and another, with a superb bird's-eye view of the town and harbour, dropping down to Peel. Either would have been preferable to slogging along the lifeless tarmac, but they were heading in the wrong direction. It was dreadfully hot, and when Thor wandered into the cool darkness of an old barn while I was taking photographs, I left him there.

Below, in Arrasy Forest, a gang of men were busy felling trees, and the whine of the chainsaws and the roar of the tractors intruded into the stillness and competed with a skylark singing its heart out in the blue sky above my head. There was not a breath of wind, yet in the air was a distinct tang of exhaust smoke mingled with spruce resin that had spiralled up the hillside for over half a mile on thermal currents. Out to sea a large white passenger ship, escorted by scores of gulls, was heading north, and through the binoculars I could make out the Norwegian flag flying from the stern and crowds of passengers lining the deck to stare at the magical Isle of Man. It must have looked very appealing with the afternoon sun lighting up the hills and the white surf crashing against the cliffs. Dotted over the flat calm water were several yachts lying motionless, sails limp, like discarded toys. Occasionally one would suddenly come alive and surge forward as the crew started the yacht's engine, anxious to make the most of their precious holiday.

Thor emerged from the barn and, taking it as a sign that he was ready to move on, I clipped his lead rope on and led him down to Glenmaye village. The only way to reach Dalby and the Watersons' farm was along a busy main road carrying a steady stream of tourist traffic, and I had to keep Thor well into the side of the road to avoid being struck by half-wits who thought it great sport to try to clip the packs as they drove by.

The traffic was particularly bad on a steep hill with a series of hairpin bends rising out of the village, and by the time we reached the top I was worn out with the effort of hauling Thor to safety every time a car came too close for comfort. I had pulled into the gateway of a large house to escape from the traffic and rest when, to my surprise, a lady popped her head over the hedge and asked if Thor would like a bucket of water. I replied that there was probably nothing in the world which would give him greater pleasure at that moment, and she smiled and opened the gate to let us into the garden.

It was like a dream – one minute I was towing Thor through the traffic, and the next I was stretched out in a chair in a lovely garden clutching a cup of tea and a cake, while Thor stood in the shade of a large sycamore tree guzzling a bucket of sparkling water. The lady's husband joined us and said they had watched us slogging up the hill in the heat and thought we might appreciate a drink. We talked about the increase in traffic on the island, and he said he remembered the days when the main road was so quiet it was possible to turn cows onto it. There had been a water-mill in Glenmaye, and farmers used to pass by the house regularly with horse-drawn carts loaded with sacks of corn for the mill.

'In those days there were some real old characters,' said the man, smiling at the memory. 'There used to be a house on that first hairpin bend coming out of the village. An old chap called Nick used to live in the top half, and underneath he kept cows and hens, and always had a line of wooden troughs for feeding them spread out on the road in front of the house. He was a cantankerous old devil and was always feuding with the farmers because they complained about the troughs being stuck right on the bend, but he wouldn't shift them. One local farmer got the measure of him though! Every time he came along with his horse and cart, he deliberately ran a wheel over the troughs and flattened them. Nick used to go wild, but the farmer always had the excuse that he couldn't stop the horse on the hill.' The man drained his cup and placed it on the garden table. 'You could fill a book about Manx characters like Nick, but you'd have to move fast; there aren't many left who remember them.'

It was so pleasant sitting in the lovely garden chatting with such a friendly couple that I could have stayed all day, but there was still another two miles of main road to negotiate to Dalby and I wanted to get the ordeal over with. Thor was as reluctant to leave as I, but refreshed and rested we faced the traffic with renewed energy. I learnt later that my kind friends were Margaret and William Quirk, and William was a member of the Manx Parliament. It would be nice if Westminster MPs would lean over their garden gates and invite perfect strangers in for tea!

The walk along the main road turned out to be more enjoyable than I had anticipated. There was not a car to be seen all the way to Dalby, and it was a delight to wander peacefully along, enjoying the view of the coastline and listening to the calls of the sea birds.

Creglea Farm was marked on the Ordnance Survey map almost on the edge of the sea cliffs and was easy to find, but when I arrived in the farmyard there was no sign of life. I banged on the porch door and shouted, but there was no answer, and I was about to turn away when I spotted a note pinned to the wall outside the porch. It read: 'Bob Orrell. Sorry we're out but go in and make yourself at home. There's coffee in the cupboard, milk in the fridge, and cakes in the tin by the kettle. Back soon.' It was a lovely, hospitable gesture, and on an island where there is comparatively little crime it must be very comforting to be able to leave your house open without fear of some no-good helping himself to the contents.

The Isle of Man Government has long been the target of intense criticism for its policy of birching offenders but has steadfastly refused to alter its penal code. Opponents of corporal punishment argue that it is degrading and barbaric. Manx people counter by saying that for those very reasons it is an effective deterrent to the hooligan element, and compare the almost negligible amount of violent crime on the island with the horrifying statistics of wanton destruction and brutal attacks on old people, women and children that have become almost a way of life on mainland Britain. It is an emotive subject, but in an age when we vehemently defend democracy, is it not the first rule of the game that the majority decision of the people is the one that is recognized?

I unloaded Thor and turned him into a field near the house, and he immediately sank to his knees as if sending up a prayer of thanks for deliverance from the unrelenting weight of the saddle and packs. Normally during a journey the weight of the packs gradually decreases as I use up my stock of food, but on the island the people I stayed with were so hospitable and generous that my packets of dehydrated delicacies were hardly touched. The prayer over, Thor was soon on his feet again, and it was good to see him galloping round the field like a youngster. For a pony in his twenty-third year, he was remarkably fit.

It was a nice feeling to be trusted by people I had never met in my life, and I went into the big farm kitchen, made a cup of coffee and sat on the field gate sharing a chunk of the Watersons' home-made cake with Thor. There was not a cloud in the sky, and with the sun highlighting buildings and trees, the conditions were ideal for photography, so when we had eaten I grabbed my cameras and walked back to look at the village of Dalby.

In *A six days tour in the Isle of Man* published in 1836, the author described Dalby as 'the fag end of a God-forgotten world', but he was being unfair to what is quite an attractive corner of the island. Certainly the village – if a straggle of houses, a church and a hotel can be classified as a village – is not the most inspiring of places, but the scenery around it is superb.

Visitors now drive through Dalby and barely give it a second glance, but at the beginning of the present century 'The Dalby Outrages' were front-page news throughout Britain. A series of killings and horrible maimings of cattle and horses on a farm near the village were thought at first to be a vendetta against the farmer but, though rumours and suspicions spread like wildfire, nothing could ever be proved. Fires were started in the farm buildings, and the domestic water supply, which was kept under lock and key, was contaminated with the carcase of a dead sheep. The attacks were spread over several years and became so serious that policemen were stationed at the farm, yet they continued, and one fire was started while the police were actually guarding the building. Detectives came over from the mainland to help with investigations but, though they stayed for several months, they found nothing. The strain and worry were too much for the unfortunate farmer and, broken in mind and health, he died. Immediately the attacks on the farm ceased.

The Dalby Outrages have long intrigued those who enjoy delving into the supernatural, but whether it was the work of a demon spirit or simply a vindictive neighbour who always managed to keep one step ahead of the police is still an unsolved mystery.

With the departure of the police and the reporters, Dalby rapidly faded from the limelight, but the villagers' peace was short lived, for in the 1930s news of Gef, the 'talking weasel' who had befriended thirteen-year-old Voirrey Irving and lived on top of a cupboard in her bedroom, sent droves of newspapermen back to the island. The Irvings lived at Doarlish Cashen, a bleak farm in the hills above Dalby. They were wakened one night by mysterious thumpings behind the wood panelling of one of the bedrooms, and the sound of an animal growling and spitting. The terrifying noise kept the family awake night after night, but instead of being driven away from the house they began to talk to the 'creature', and feed it bits of chocolate and banana. It became increasingly friendly with Voirrey, and when she persuaded it to run across a beam in the house, the family saw an animal that looked like a ferret but which had a long bushy tail like a squirrel. Mrs Irving stroked its tail and back and discovered that its front feet resembled a human hand with three or four fingers and a thumb, which 'gripped her fingers as in a vice'. The story might have ended there had it not been for the animal's ability to speak several languages, sing songs and hymns, throw stones at 'doubters' who did not believe in it and kill rabbits for the family dinner.

Hard on the heels of the newspapermen came representatives from the Council for Psychical Investigation and the National Laboratory of Psychical Research, Spiritualists and scores of others with an interest in occultism, witchcraft and magic. Many of them dismissed Gef as a hoax and hinted that Voirrey was a clever ventriloquist. Mediums insisted that Gef was nothing more than a spirit, until it was pointed out that spirits are seldom partial to large helpings of potato pie, rabbit stew, chocolate and bananas. The Psychic Researchers took a more serious interest in Voirrey's pet and decided it was a form of mongoose. A number of distinguished investigators paid several visits to Doarlish Cashen and sat for hours waiting for Gef to appear but, apart from a voice abusing them from behind the wood panelling, they had little to report. They even gave Voirrey a camera, hoping for a photograph of the elusive Gef, but the figure on the photographs she took was only an unrecognizable blob on a grassy bank. Eventually enthusiasm for the elusive and camera-shy Gef waned, and after four years newspaper editors withdrew their journalists, proving as they do on so many occasions that rumour sells more newspapers than a reliable report.

The whole story of Gef, Voirrey and the Irving family is told in a fascinating book called *The Haunting of Cashen's Gap* by H. Price and R.S. Lambert.

Had the Irvings been able to show a reliable photograph of Gef, or better still produce him in the flesh, he would have been a major tourist attraction and undoubtedly the Irvings would have made a fortune. It is sad for them that few believed the story of the Dalby 'spook', but at least the island has been spared a plethora of Gef souvenirs – Gef T-shirts, woolly hats and jigsaw puzzles.

The Watersons were at home when I got back to the farm, and they made me very welcome and insisted I stay the night in the house. Margaret said that, if I really wanted to see Manx scenery at its finest, I should not miss the opportunity to visit Niarbyl since I was so close, and said she would take me there.

The Isle of Man is full of surprises, but I never expected to find anything as unusual as Niarbyl. It was only a quarter of a mile or so from the farm along a narrow road that seemed to go straight off the edge of the cliffs into the sea but at the last minute veered left and zigzagged down to a rocky cove hidden from view. A sprinkling of rocks and small islands protected it from the sea, and a great cave went deep into the rock. Tucked under the shelter of the cliffs, above the shingle beach, was a whitewashed cottage with a thatched roof and an upturned boat and lobster-pots stacked against the wall. It was like stepping back a century into a smuggler's hide-away, and at any moment I expected to see a line of figures troop out of the cave, cutlasses stuffed in waistbands, casks of rum on their shoulders. The timeless scene was rather spoilt by the presence of the inevitable gift shop, but even that had a rustic charm, and I bought a couple of pendants made of shells to take home for my daughters.

At dinner that evening we were sitting round the table talking when a vehicle pulled into the yard and Frank Keig appeared at the door, bursting with excitement.

'I've got Lucy for you,' he cried. 'Come and help me unload.'

I was out of the house in a flash and flung my arms round Lucy's neck. Thor saw her too, and I thought he would smash the fence to pieces as he raced up and down, whinnying and kicking his heels up in the air. I felt I was intruding on a tender love scene when I led Lucy into the field. They kissed and snickered, rubbed each other's necks, raced round and round, then kissed and snickered all over again before finally settling down to lie together as the evening sun slanted across the field. It was very beautiful to watch and, though cynics would dismiss it as simply an example of herding instinct, I have lived with ponies enough to know that they can become inseparably attached to each other. They may not be able to express the depth of feeling two people can show for each other, but I am sure that when separated from their closest companion they experience the same sensations of pain.

We went back into the kitchen and, while Donald handed round cans of beer, Frank explained that John Huyton had phoned from Grenaby with the news that the vet had said Lucy was fit for work, and he had driven over right away to collect her. The painful limp had been caused by a pulled tendon in the lower half of her leg, and the few days of rest had reduced the swelling. The vet had said that, provided she was not worked too hard, she would be fine.

After Frank had departed for home, I spread the map out on the kitchen table to plan the next day's route. I wanted to visit Port St Mary, Port Erin and Calf Island, but in the south of the island quiet tracks were few and far between and, though I pored over the map with a magnifying glass, it was clear that the only way I could travel south was along main roads.

'You could try the Fishermen's Road,' suggested Donald, 'but I walked part of it recently and it was very boggy where it climbs up the hill.' He pointed to a track on the map that ran from Dalby to a little hamlet at Cregganmoar but thereafter was marked as a path climbing directly up a steep hillside by a forest plantation to continue as a track again for two miles before joining a main road leading to Port St Mary.

'It's a very ancient route,' explained Donald. 'In the days of sail, if the weather was bad and the Port St Mary fishermen couldn't get round the Calf after fishing off the west of the island, they used to leave their boats in Peel and walk home. Since then it's always been known as the Fishermen's Road. When you look at the map, you can see how the modern road-builders followed the line of the old route, but the bit from Cregganmoar must have been too steep, so they contoured round Dalby mountain.'

Traversing steep, rocky ground would not have presented any difficulty with two fit ponies, but with the vet's warning about not pushing Lucy too hard ringing in my ears it would have been silly to have taken her up a steep hillside just for the sake of avoiding the main road. I compromised by deciding to follow the gently rising main road for two miles, which nicely avoided the steep path from Cregganmoar, then join the Fishermen's Road higher up, at Eary Cushlin. Thereafter I would have three miles of peaceful track before facing the ordeal of six miles of busy main road to Port St Mary.

Decision made, I went to bed, my head buzzing with excitement at having Lucy back again, but slightly apprehensive about the sort of welcome I would get from the people in the south of the island. When I asked my friend who lived in Cumberland what the islanders were like to get on with, she said: 'Like anywhere else, there's good and bad among them, but you might find that the people in the south are a bit less inclined to stop and talk to you than those in the north. It's not that they're any less friendly, but they are more geared up for tourists. It might be difficult to get grazing for your ponies and a place to camp – and by the way, on the island we talk about "down north" and "up south" when we are giving directions, so you'll just have to get used to it.'

9

Kettle and the Calf of Man

At breakfast, the weatherman on the Watersons' radio gleefully announced that it would be another shorts-and-T-shirt day and that the hot weather looked set to continue for another week at least.

'There will be sighs of relief all round at that news,' said Donald, spreading marmalade on a piece of toast. 'Tynwald Day isn't far off, and the ceremony at St John's is a marvellous spectacle if it's a nice sunny day.'

The conversation turned to the vagaries of the British weather, and I said it was lovely to have such gorgeous weather, but if it was like that all the time the island would soon become unbelievably crowded. Without rain the hills wouldn't have the lovely colours and would be bleached and lifeless as in some of the Mediterranean countries.

'You're quite right,' agreed Donald, 'but we have such an unpredictable climate that when the rain starts it sometimes forgets to stop for a week or two, and if it happens to coincide with somebody's holiday they go away vowing never to come back.'

The clamour of the telephone bell in the hallway brought the conversation to an abrupt end, and I went out to load the ponies.

Having spent several days on John Huyton's lush grass, Lucy had put on a lot of weight, so I had to let out the pack-saddle girth to the last notch before I could get it to fit round her stomach, and even then it was a struggle, but by ten o'clock we were ready. With a final wave to the

116

Watersons, I steered Thor out onto the road and, with Lucy ambling behind, headed for Dalby.

I get a lot of pleasure from walking, but it was very pleasant to be back in the saddle again and feel Thor's powerful muscles propelling him forward. The forward motion never challenged any speed records, and it was all the better for that. It gave me a chance to relax and enjoy the view, jot an occasional note in my diary and snap a photograph or two. If the pace slackened or I thought the ponies were becoming bored with the long slog along the road, reviving flagging energy was a simple matter of leaning forward with half a Mars bar for Thor and backwards with a similar incentive for Lucy.

In this delightfully unhurried way we left Dalby behind and zigzagged up along the side of Dalby mountain, to emerge on a plateau with an extensive view of the rocky coastline, nearly a thousand feet below, on one side, and the great gash of Glen Rushen on the other. It was hot, but not unbearable; the sky was a deep blue, with matching sea; and really it was the sort of day when a string of superlatives was inadequate – one word was sufficient: 'perfect'. And not a solitary car had passed us all the way from Dalby.

On the plateau the motor road cut across an old track that had come over Dalby mountain from Glenmaye, and at this point we left the tarmac in favour of the stony surface of a mile or two of Manx history into which a pack pony fitted perfectly. For a short distance the track kept close to the edge of the Kerroodhoo forest plantation, then swung left at the entrance to the Manx National Trust's wild expanse of moor, trees and sea cliffs at Eary Cushlin, where, according to an intriguing leaflet pinned to a post, 'ramblage' was permitted. 'Ramblage' was a word I had never before encountered, and there was no indication to what extent one could ramblage, or whether it was confined to the period between sunrise and sunset, allowed on Sundays or permitted only between consenting adults!

Lucy was out of condition through over-eating and lack of exercise during her enforced rest, and to ease the strain

I let her stop as often as she wanted to, and reduced the weight of the packs by transferring as many heavy items as I could into Thor's saddlebags. It was only after having stopped more times than seemed necessary along the track from Eary Cushlin that I realized the crafty little devil had worked out that if she stopped I would make a fuss of her, give her two or three mints and take more weight out of the packs.

All too soon the enjoyable ride along the old track came to an end and we were back on the main road, but at least it was all downhill, which made it easier on the ponies, and the view was fabulous. The entire sweep of the coast from Spanish Head on the west, along by Port St Mary, Castletown and Derby Haven to the low promontory of Langness, lay spread out like a relief map. At Ronaldsway Airport, by Castletown, aircraft were arriving like bees returning to a nest, or taking off to circle the airport before settling on a course for London, Blackpool, Liverpool, Dublin or Belfast. Every detail of Calf Island and the tower of the lighthouse on the foam-lashed Chicken Rock was crystal clear. With the aid of a powerful telephoto lens I could have captured some superb shots, but there has to be a limit to what is carried on a horseback journey, and my policy is to take only the absolute minimum of photographic equipment.

Photography is a very popular pastime, but to carry all the essentials recommended by some photography books would require a train of camels. I find that two Pentax 35mm cameras fitted with 28-75 zoom lenses, a lightweight tripod, a small flashgun, lens hoods, a small changing bag (in case a film jams) and a few filters are quite adequate. The only other essential is a thoroughly waterproof camera bag.

Using a convenient road sign as a camera rest, I took a series of photographs of Calf Island and Port St Mary, and then continued on down the hill. Lucy was sweating profusely, and her body was so wet that the pack-saddle girth kept slipping. It was a sign that a long rest was called for to cool off, and by a stroke of fortune the pack saddle finally slid off Lucy's back as we reached a roadside sheep

pen with a large fenced paddock. It was an ideal place to
stop and, with the ponies enjoying a well-earned rest, I
spread the saddle blanket along a fence to dry, then set
about assembling the stove and preparing a meal of packet
soup, fortified with croutons and Ryvita biscuits, followed
by a mug of coffee and a delicious bar of compressed oats,
honey and apple flakes. Lying in the sun listening to the
sounds of the countryside and Thor and Lucy grazing in
the paddock was wonderfully peaceful and, unable to keep
my eyes open, I fell fast asleep.

Two hours later I woke with a start to find a policeman
standing over me, coughing politely.

'Sorry to wake you,' he grinned. 'We had a report from a
passing motorist that there was a body lying by the side of
the road. But you look pretty healthy to me!'

I rubbed the sleep out of my eyes and got to my feet. 'A
body?' I repeated incredulously. 'How could anyone be
silly enough to report a body?'

'Don't worry about it,' he laughed. 'People report the
strangest things. It was an elderly lady who saw you as she
drove by, and was afraid to stop. We had to check.' He
walked over to look at the ponies. 'Where are you making
for?' he asked. I told him about my journey, and that I was
hoping to find a farm where I could camp in Port St Mary.
He rubbed his chin thoughtfully. 'Try Robert Cooil at
Ballacreggan Farm. He's an obliging sort of chap. You
can't miss it. Third set of crossroads at the bottom of the
hill.' He pencilled a few lines in his notebook and nodded
towards Thor and Lucy staring at him over the fence. 'One
thing's for sure. You're not likely to get done for speeding
with these two,' he joked. 'Hope the weather keeps fine for
you.' I heard him report on his patrol car radio that the
'body' was alive and well, and then with a wave he drove
off.

Port St Mary is a very popular tourist centre, and on the
outskirts of the town coaches and cars poured from every
direction in a never-ending stream, making the ponies
very jumpy. Coach-drivers were the greatest worry,
hurling their chrome-plated monsters along at full speed
as if they were competing with each other for a coveted

trophy, awarded to the first driver to get his passengers to the coach-park toilets.

Ballacreggan Farm was easy to find and, having overcome the initial shock of seeing a pack pony in their yard, Robert Cooil and his wife Doreen were full of welcome.

'Put the ponies in the field behind the barn,' said Robert, 'and when you've got the tent pitched, come up to the house and have some tea with us.'

The field was huge and, rid of their loads, Thor and Lucy set off on their usual end-of-the-day celebration gallop, pursued by a herd of inquisitive cattle. I pitched the tent in a sheltered corner well away from the mad stampede, spread the saddles along the fence and went back to the farmhouse. The kitchen table was heaped with food, and I sat down with the family and tucked in to an enormous meal.

'We're going out for a drink later on,' said Robert. 'Would you like to come with us? We usually go down to a pub by the harbour, and if Kettle's there he'll fill you up with a few tales!'

'Who on earth is "Kettle"?' I asked.

Doreen smiled. 'Oh, he's a fisherman,' she said. 'That isn't his real name, but everyone knows him as Kettle. You'll enjoy talking to him.'

When the meal was over, I went back to the tent to capture a shot of the sun setting behind Bradda Head and later, with hair combed and shoes freshly dubbined, I crammed into the Cooils' car for the short run into the town.

The pub was packed to the door with a boisterous crowd of customers, but we managed to wedge ourselves into a corner by the bar, and a pint of beer was thrust into my hand by Doreen's father, George, who lives at the farm with them. Robert bellowed to someone in another room, and a man holding his glass of beer above his head pushed his way through the crowd and joined us.

'This is Kettle,' said Robert, introducing him. 'He'll tell you anything you want to know about Manx fishing and the sea.'

We shook hands and I took an immediate liking to him. He was typical of fishermen to be found in any port in Britain – rough and tough but warm-hearted and generous. They are a breed of men who endure the most incredible hardships and dangers and are at the mercy of wildly fluctuating fish prices, hounded by bureaucracy and treated with only perfunctory interest by politicians. Yet they do not demand a lot from life. Kettle's main concern was that diesel fuel was a lot more expensive on the island than on the British mainland or in Ireland, so other fleets had an advantage over Manx boats. He said the high cost of fuel and the shortage of fish had made many fishermen sell their boats and get out of fishing, and there was only a handful of Manx-registered boats left.

'We used to sing about the herring being King of the Sea,' said Kettle, 'but not any more.'

Robert elbowed his way to our corner with a fistful of pint glasses overflowing with beer. 'Get these down you,' he ordered. 'Talking is thirsty work! There's another two ready on the bar when you've finished.' He turned to Kettle. 'Have you told him about the time when you used to take stores out to Chicken Rock?'

'There isn't a lot to tell, really,' said Kettle. He drained his glass and picked up a full one from the bar. 'I suppose you'll know of the Chicken Rock lighthouse?' I nodded. 'Well,' he continued, 'it's a hell of a place even in good weather, what with the strong tide that races round those rocks, and we got the contract to take coal and stores out for the keepers. We thought we were on to a good thing, but by God we had a few frights! There's always a big swell round there, and trying to land sacks of coal and boxes of food on the Rock without losing any or wrecking the boat was a nightmare. In the winter some of those seas would frighten the life out of you, and all for a few pounds a week. It came to an end when the tower went on fire and they made it an automatic light. You ought to take a run out to Calf Island while you're here. You'll get a good view of Chicken Rock, and the island's an interesting place to wander round.'

I said I was planning to go out to Calf Island the

following day on a boat from Port Erin if the weather was fine.

'Don't worry yourself about the weather,' Kettle assured me. 'The glass is high and steady. It'll be another sunny day tomorrow.' He glanced at his watch, then hastily finished his drink. 'I've got to be off,' he said. 'I'm taking a party of surveyors out in the boat tomorrow, and it's an early start. Enjoy your stay, and make sure you give us fishermen a mention if you write anything!'

The crowd at the bar parted to let him through, then closed together in a rush for last orders before closing time.

When we left the pub, darkness was settling over the harbour. Black silhouettes of moored boats stood motionless on a flat calm sea. It was a warm, balmy evening, and the picturesque harbour front of Port St Mary had a flavour of a French or Spanish fishing port, but there the similarity ended. There were no quayside cafés lit by lanterns, where the clink of glasses and happy laughter mingled with the romantic sound of an accordion or guitar. There was no aroma of steak being grilled on open-air barbecues, or the tang of lobster and fresh-cooked fish wafting up from a cellar bistro. No lovers walked hand in hand along the pavement or lingered over a glass of wine at a parasoled table. The island's licensing laws permit no such Continental decadence, and as the pub doors banged shut, the last café hung up its 'closed' sign, the fat cooled in the darkened fish and chip shop, and the village clock chimed a curfew over deserted streets.

I woke in the night with a raging headache, and a dose of Paracetamol did little to ease the pain. According to the packet, the contents were a powerful cure for all headaches, but the company had obviously never tested its product against Isle of Man ale! Unable to sleep, I lit the stove to make coffee and sat in the open door of the tent, hoping that a mixture of caffeine and chilly morning air might have more effect than medical science. The first streaks of dawn were beginning to break the horizon, and all round the tent the dew-soaked grass shone like a sea of tarnished silver. Weird forms swathed in streamers of mist lay on the surface, smoke billowing from their nostrils like some grotesque creatures of the deep, but as the sun rose and spirited away the mist, the threatening shadows were transformed into the familiar figures of Thor and Lucy, close together on the grass.

It was the start of a lovely day and, dashing down a quick breakfast of muesli mixed with condensed milk, I packed my rucksack with food and cameras and walked to Port Erin to catch the boat to Calf Island.

Sea conditions were perfect for a cruise, but the boat was packed with a party of Senior Citizens on holiday from Leeds who either mistrusted the weather forecasts or were convinced that, having exceeded the age of sixty-five, it was fatal to expose any part of the anatomy to the elements, even at the height of a heatwave. They were swathed in thick coats, hats, scarves, gloves, Wellington boots and in some cases suits of oilskins, complete with sou'westers. Even at ten-thirty in the morning the temperature was already climbing towards 20°C but they stoically endured the discomfort, and not so much as a glove or a scarf was removed.

The temperature under a dozen tweed caps and woolly hats soared a few more degrees when, as the boat was about to pull away from the quay, two pretty girls in their early twenties stepped on board dressed only in the briefest of bikinis. The minute pieces of material were no more than a token concession to decency, and there was an almost audible hiss of disapproval from the ladies. They tried every trick in the book to concentrate the attention of their menfolk on the formation of the cliffs, the gulls, the sea, jellyfish, a plastic bottle floating in the water – anything at all to distract them from the Jezebels draped along the side of the boat, but they were fighting a losing battle. With glazed eyes and rasping breath, the old chaps gazed in stunned disbelief at the two beauties, and they looked so ill that when the skipper reached for his radio-telephone I felt he was about to call the coastguard to evacuate six suspected heart-attacks and a possible stroke case, but he merely reported the boat's position.

Those who watch over us ended the crisis by whipping up a sudden breeze that had the girls rushing to open their rucksacks and scramble into shirts and jeans. As quick as it arrived, the breeze died, and it was as hot as ever. The power of elderly female prayer is mighty!

The tide was running very strongly through Kitterland Sound, between the southern tip of Man and Calf Island, and for a few minutes the boat was thrown about like a cork, but we were soon through it into calmer waters and nosed into South Harbour, a narrow natural inlet in the rock where the lighthouse authority had built a concrete jetty. The skipper said he would pick us up at Cow Harbour at the opposite end of the island, and I leapt ashore to get well ahead of the crowd and climbed a rough path to the summit of a low hill carpeted with pink thrift.

Wild Loaghton sheep with tangled horns wandered among the rocks, and there were birds everywhere. In the short distance from the jetty I saw puffins, chough, cormorants, herring gulls, fulmars and oyster-catchers, with many more I could not identify. The rocky coast was a jumble of scattered inlets and coves where a turquoise sea rose and fell, throwing columns of white spume into the air that flashed in the sun and fell back in a lather of foam. It was unbelievably beautiful, and I sat on a rock spellbound by the scenery and the view of the Chicken Rock lighthouse close inshore.

Calf Island is one of those chunks of rock which, on landing, you either see only as a desolate, windswept wilderness and enquire when the next boat leaves for the mainland, or are immediately captivated by and hope you will miss the boat and have to stay for ever. It is only 1½ miles long by one mile wide, but far from being flat and uninteresting, the north end rises to 421 feet, with spectacular cliffs alive with sea birds climbing vertically out of the sea. The name 'Calf' has nothing to do with farm animals; it is from the Norse '*kalfr*', meaning a small island close to a larger one.

As on its larger neighbour, one of Calf Island's early residents paddled his boat across from Ireland to spread

the Christian message. He found the tranquillity of the
Calf very much to his liking and is reputed to have lived
there for many years and actually built a chapel, though its
location has never been identified. In the sixteenth
century the island was a favourite haven for fugitives from
justice, and one story tells of a nobleman who, having
killed a woman in a fit of rage and jealousy, escaped to the
Calf to live the life of a hermit and devote his time to
prayer. His reluctance to tell anyone his name, however,
has left historians wondering if the tale might be more
folklore than fact.

A century later, when Thomas Bushell fell foul of King
James and hot-footed it to hide in a cave on Calf Island, he
told the locals it was just a rest cure: 'I have resolved to
make a perfect experiment upon myself for the obtaining
of a long and healthy life, most necessary for such a
repentance as my former debauchedness required, by a
parsimonious diet of herbs, oil, mustard and honey, with
water sufficient ...' He survived the sparse diet and
vigorous climate but yearned for the high life and after
'three years unsociable solitude, in ye desolated isle called
the Calf of Man' returned to London where, at the end of
a fascinating life, he died at the age of eighty and was
buried in Westminster Abbey.

When the Earl of Derby tried to establish deer on the
Calf in the eighteenth century, and failed, he unwittingly
became the world's first rabbit farmer – though, had
anybody pointed it out to him at the time, they might well
have ended up dangling from the end of a rope. While the
deer declined to go forth and multiply, the rabbits had no
such inhibitions, and within a short time of being
introduced to the island they swarmed in their thousands.
Rather than use them for idle target practice for their
hunting friends, successive earls realized they were a cash
crop and to safeguard their investment decreed, '... that
no manner of person or persons whatever, shall presume
to go unto the Calf Isle by day or night ... to annoy destroy
and carry away the Lord's game there, under the penalty
of forfeiting the sum of three pounds sterling ... and to
endure such punishment as the offence will deserve'.

Over the centuries the island was developed as a sheep farm, and root crops were introduced, but the rabbit ruled, and though thousands were killed and shipped away to the mainland, they continued to breed and it was impossible to keep them in check. One farmer and his family were so sick of eating rabbit that at mealtimes they prayed:

> For rabbits hot and rabbits cold
> For rabbits young and rabbits old,
> For rabbits tender, rabbits tough,
> I thank the Lord I've had enough.

Another rapid-breeding but considerably less delectable rodent was an even greater menace to the farmers and their families. In 1786, when a Russian ship was wrecked close to the island, the rats on board swam ashore and infested the island as thickly as the rabbits. It must have needed a strong nerve to live where thousands of rats swarmed like ants around the buildings, and not until modern science produced an effective poison were they contained and finally eliminated. The evil of man's myxomatosis put paid to the rabbits.

It might well have been Manannan MacLir, the first ruler of Man, who, still guarding the Isle of Man from his throne in the sky, saw the greatest threat to the future of the Calf since the arrival of the Vikings. Disguised as Francis Dickens, a Lancashire businessman, he boarded a train to Manchester in time to prevent Joshua Appleyard Popplewell selling the island to a company which planned to develop it as a tourist attraction. If that version of events is too fanciful for the pragmatist to swallow, perhaps the account given by W. Lockington Marshall in his book *The Calf of Man* might be more acceptable.

Joshua Appleyard Popplewell of Arnside, Lancashire (now part of Cumbria), bought the Calf in 1931 because he thought the air would be beneficial to his son, who was suffering from tuberculosis. He spent a lot of money improving living-conditions on the island, even to the extent of installing a telephone, but the strong tide kept damaging the cable and it was eventually abandoned.

When Popplewell had lived on the Calf for about five years, while on a visit to Lancashire he boarded a Manchester train and found himself sharing a carriage with Francis Joseph Dickens, an old friend. Dickens was a great lover of the Isle of Man and during the course of the conversation was horrified to discover that Popplewell had almost completed a deal to sell the island to a company that wanted to exploit it as a tourist attraction. He promptly offered Popplewell £500 more than the company's bid, and to his delight it was accepted. But while the technicality of buying the Calf presented no problem, when he wanted to give it away gratis he found himself confronted with an obstacle he had not anticipated. He very generously gifted the island to the English National Trust only to discover that the Trust had no power to acquire or administer land in the Isle of Man. He had to take his case to the House of Lords, where a new Act of Parliament was passed, but with the proviso '... always that the Trust shall not be exercised with reference to any property situate in the Isle of Man without the approval of Tynwald ...'

At the time Tynwald could do little else than approve the acquisition, since the Isle of Man had no National Trust of its own. The English National Trust appointed a Warden and administered the island until 1951, when they granted a twenty-one year lease to the newly formed Manx Museum and National Trust, at an annual rent of £1. Taking on the lease meant being responsible for all the expense of maintaining the farm buildings and paying the Warden's wages, and it caused a few ripples of dissent among the members of the House of Keys. After all, they argued, why should the Manx taxpayers maintain the property of an English owner, even if it was the National Trust? Privately they vowed that one day the Calf would be returned to its rightful owners, the people of Man.

On 6 November 1986 the dream came true, when the National Trust of England and Wales handed over the ownership of the Calf of Man to the Manx Museum and National Trust, for all time, in exchange for a token payment of a Manx gold noble. Manannan MacLir, with a little help from the English, had won another battle!

The other passengers from the boat had streamed past me and disappeared from view when I set off to explore the island, and I felt I had it all to myself. There was so much I wanted to see but, with only two hours to spend before the boat returned, I had to make a quick decision and opted to visit the lighthouse first, then go on to the farm.

With three lighthouses grouped close together on the headland, and a fourth sticking out of the sea nearby, the west side of the Calf looks rather like a lighthouse testing range, but each one is an important chapter in the maritime history of the Isle of Man. With its outlying rocks and fierce tides the Calf of Man was dreaded by seamen and shipowners, and hundreds of ships were wrecked and their crews lost. For over forty years the Lord of Man, the Duke of Atholl, ignored requests for a lighthouse to be built on the Calf, until, threatened with the wrath of the Northern Lighthouse Board, he reluctantly agreed. The greatest hazard was not so much the Calf itself as the partly submerged Chicken Rock to the south, and Robert Stevenson, of the famous Stevenson family of lighthouse engineers, hit on the idea of building two lighthouses, one slightly higher than the other, so that when they were in line they pointed to the position of the Rock. The twin lights first flashed out their warning in February 1818, but they were often obscured if clouds were low, and ships continued to disappear off the Calf. Liverpool ship-owners besieged the Board of Trade for a light on Chicken Rock, and eventually the Stevensons returned and built another of their hundred-foot masterpieces in the swirling tides three-quarters of a mile offshore. On New Year's Day 1875 the lamp was lit for the first time, and simultaneously the two lights on the Calf were extinguished for ever.

There were now two abandoned lighthouses on the Calf and one manned by keepers on the Chicken Rock, but after a disastrous fire in 1960, during which the keepers escaped by sliding down a rope from the top of the tower, the great Stevenson monument was put out of action, and after repairs to the structure an unmanned light of greatly reduced power was established in 1962.

After 140 years and three lighthouses, the Calf was still without a light powerful enough to be an effective warning, but the Northern Lighthouse Board were not to be beaten! A brand-new lighthouse was built on the Calf near the site of the earlier lighthouses, beaming 2 million candlepower twenty-three miles out into the Irish Sea. Compared with the solid granite towers of the Stevenson era, the new square lighthouse building looks almost fragile, but to the men who spend their lives tending the light it is sheer luxury.

'A damned sight better than living in that drainpipe on the Chicken Rock,' commented one of the keepers when I asked what he thought of the new building, 'and it's great being on the Calf! When you're off watch, you can go for a walk, and there's always a few visitors and ornithologists to have a yarn with. It lets you feel you're still part of life.'

He showed me round the engine room and radio station and proudly demonstrated the modern gadgetry. Lighthouses have come a long way since the early days of wick lamps and clockwork mechanisms, but ironically the same advance in technology will eventually make the lighthouse-keeper's job obsolete. More and more lighthouses are being converted to unmanned automatic lights, and in the not too distant future, when sophisticated electronic position-finders will be fitted to even the smallest boat, the beacons that have guided mariners for centuries will no longer be needed. Like the Colosseum of the Romans and the Greek Parthenon, our lighthouses will stand gaunt and empty, the crumbling edifices of a once great maritime nation.

I used up a whole film photographing the lighthouses for posterity, then walked across the island to the farmhouse, tucked away on the side of a hill well sheltered from the winter gales. In the fields there were lots of relics of the island's farming days: an old cornmill, roofless and derelict, its millstones lying where they had fallen, and beautifully built walls enclosing fields once painstakingly tilled but now overgrown with chest-high bracken.

A young chap, busy working on an arrangement of netted birdtraps near the farmhouse, was very friendly and explained that the Warden had gone to another part of the island with a visitor, but offered to show me round.

The farmhouse served as accommodation for the Wardens and visiting naturalists but, though it had lost little of the atmosphere of the days when it was a working farmhouse, it was not the house but the implement sheds that I found the most exciting. The doors were nailed up and, when the assistant prised them open and we peered inside, it was as if the last farmer had decided one morning that he was sick of struggling to make a living on the island and, stopping only to hammer nails in the shed doors, had taken his family and left on the next boat. Inside one shed was an old tractor still in working order, a trailer, hay mowers and a binder. Scythes, rakes and other tools hung on hooks on the walls, and two rusting milk churns, oil drums and broken implements were scattered about the floor. Tragically, the roof of an adjoining shed had partially fallen in, and the weather had ruined a lovely old farm cart and destroyed a set of harness. I was appalled that the guardians of Manx heritage could have allowed irreplaceable links with the island's agricultural past to deteriorate in such a way!

When we returned to the house, the Warden had arrived back and I was surprised to find that his visitor was Laurence Harwood, the English National Trust's Director for the North of England, who has his offices in Ambleside in the Lake District. As a journalist I had interviewed him on several occasions and unlike many National Trust officials, who float on an elevated plane far removed from the realities of life, had found him to be a man with a genuine concern for the countryside.

The assistant Warden appeared with a tray of tea and biscuits and we all sat in the garden, relaxing in the sun and putting the world to rights. Laurence said his ongoing problem was that, as the largest landowner in the Lake District, the National Trust had somehow to maintain a balance between the needs of its farm tenants and the demands of the ever-increasing number of visitors who flocked to enjoy the Lakeland hills. There was no simple solution, but he believed that the Trust's decision to employ local rangers had contributed enormously to helping visitors understand the farmers' difficulties, and in convincing farmers that not all visitors were potential vandals.

The Warden's main concern was the effect pesticides were having on wildlife. He said he would like to see a ban on all toxic chemicals used in agriculture and that, if the people who encouraged the use of these poisons could see the pain and suffering they caused, they might stir themselves to do something about it.

'If their own pet dog or cat was poisoned by a neighbour, they would be shouting for the police,' he said, 'but a farmer can wipe out birds, mammals and insects, and nobody bats an eyelid.'

Time shot by, and when I looked at my watch I realized I had less than fifteen minutes to get to Cow Harbour for the boat to Port Erin. Gulping my tea, I shook hands quickly, hurled my camera bag over my shoulder and raced away down the track.

'You can't miss it,' the Warden shouted. 'The track goes right down to the landing. Goodbye!'

I reached the landing with five minutes to spare. The Senior Citizens were already aboard the boat, but there was no sign of the two girls. The skipper sounded the ship's horn impatiently and was about to leave when they appeared on the skyline, running flat out. Half a dozen eager old gents surged forward to help them aboard but were hauled back by claw-like hands clamped to their coat-tails.

'I can't get back in. Lift them aboard, can you?' the skipper yelled. Never one to refuse the orders of a ship's captain, I scooped the beauties, one at a time, off the landing and lowered them onto the seat next to me.

10

Steam Trains and the *Peggy*

The sail-training ship *Malcolm Miller* was anchored in the bay when we arrived in Port Erin, and our skipper circled his boat round her while the Senior Citizens made a fortune for Kodak, photographing the ship from all angles and ramming film after film into their cameras like cartridges at a clay-pigeon shoot.

When we landed at the quay, I realized I had left my windproof anorak at the farmhouse. One of the keepers on the Calf had said that he was due for relief the following day, so I phoned Langness Lighthouse, near Castletown, and asked them to radio the Calf and ask the keeper if he would be kind enough to bring my anorak with him. The crew of the *Malcolm Miller* were hoisting sail when I left the phone box, and it was a stirring sight to watch the scurry of activity on deck as the white sails crept up the masts and then filled as they caught the wind, and she sailed gracefully out of the bay round the high cliff of Bradda Head.

Port Erin is an intriguing hotch-potch of houses, hotels, shops and cafés, and at first glance the seafront gives an impression of Douglas in miniature, but it has considerably more charm than the island's capital. In the flowery language of the tourist brochures it is 'The jewel which crowns the lovely Manx Riviera ... It overlooks a lagoon-like bay, dominated by the rugged and majestic "Broad Headland" known in Manx as "Bradda".'

In the 1860s William Milner, head of the Liverpool safe

company, made his home in Port Erin and had visions of developing it into a major port. He spent a fortune on building a breakwater on the south side of the bay, and celebrated the laying of the foundation stone by roasting an ox and throwing a party for the townsfolk, but twenty years later a winter storm smashed his concrete dream to pieces and it was never rebuilt.

Milner's influence on Port Erin is remembered by an odd-shaped stone tower, perched on the top of Bradda Head, which is said to represent the shape of a key to a safe, and I climbed a steep path from the beach to take a closer look at it. In true Victorian style the tower was beautifully built, and a flight of stone steps inside spiralled to a platform with an incredible view of the Calf of Man, to the south, and Port Erin below. On the beach tiny figures were stretched out enjoying the sun but high on Bradda Head a chilly wind, pushed across the sky by a build-up of clouds on the horizon, foretold an imminent change of weather. Lingering only long enough to take a few photographs, I hurried down to the warmth of Port Erin and walked back to Ballacreggan.

Thor and Lucy were lying in the grass by the tent, so I shared a Mars bar with them and spread the map out to see if I could get from Port St Mary to Castletown and Langness the following day without having to dice with traffic along the busy main road, but I soon found that there was no alternative. All the tracks which had been beaten out over the centuries by the passage of animals had been taken over by the motor car.

'Why not leave the ponies where they are and go into Castletown on the train?' suggested Robert.

I had gone to the farmyard to fill buckets with water for Thor and Lucy, and Doreen had insisted I stay for dinner. Over a meal of Manx new potatoes and a roast of beef with fresh vegetables I had told them about my visit to the Calf, and how I wanted to visit Castletown on my way north again.

'It's a grand ride on the steam train,' continued Robert, 'and you wouldn't have to worry about finding another place to stay.'

I accepted his offer gratefully, and after dinner I phoned Dave Woods, who works in the Manx Government's Highways Department, and arranged to meet him in Castletown. Before leaving home I had written to him about Manx rights of way, and in the course of the correspondence he said that when I reached Castletown he would show me the site of an interesting shipwreck on Langness. Weary after a long day and lack of sleep the previous night, I borrowed a book about Manx history from Robert and returned to the tent. At the end of a sombre chapter about the influence of the Church on the island some wag had pencilled:

> Some go to church to say they've been,
> Some go to church to see and be seen.
> Some go to church to wink and nod,
> How many go to worship God?

At precisely 10.18 a.m. the following day the little green steam engine and red coaches that forms the morning train from Port Erin, stopping at Port St Mary, Castletown and all stations to Douglas, clanked and wheezed to a halt at Port St Mary station – a waiting-room and level crossing a few yards from Ballacreggan Farm. I stepped aboard and joined two other passengers on the hard seats. A whistle shrilled, the guard waved the green flag, the engine hooted an acknowledgement and chuffed forward gathering speed, and we were on our way. It was no Orient Express, but for one privileged to have been a small boy in the days of steam locomotives, and the envy of my classmates for boasting an uncle who was an engine-driver, the smell of steam evoked many happy memories of riding on the hotplate and helping to stoke the fire as we chugged between Crewe and Market Drayton on a hot summer's day.

The train rattled and swayed along at a remarkable speed, and I lay against the seat back and watched the countryside unfold as the line curved inland through a latticework of meadows, and pondered on the thought that, had it not been for Milner building his breakwater at

Port Erin, there might not have been a railway on the island
at all. Businessmen realized that when the breakwater was
completed Port Erin would become an important steamer
terminal, and plans were immediately made to form a
railway company. The rail network spread all over the
island, but as roads improved and vehicles became more
widely used, the railway was gradually used less and less,
until all that remains is the line from Port Erin to Douglas,
and that clings tenaciously to life only with the support of
the Manx Government.

With just one stop at Colby to pick up passengers, and an
unscheduled halt while the engine crew and the guard
chased a stray cow off the line, the journey passed all too
quickly and I was sorry I had to leave the train at Castletown
and not give it my support by staying on all the way to
Douglas. The little train was so proud of itself, with gleaming brass and polished woodwork, yet there was an air of
resignation about it as if it knew that carrying only a
handful of passengers was not enough and that more
friends and admirers were needed if it was to be saved from
the clutches of the scrap-metal merchants.

In an age when architects seem unable to think beyond
the shape of a packet of cornflakes when designing housing
estates, the planners have mercifully kept modern development well apart from the old-world charm of Castletown,
and to wander round the ancient harbour and through the
narrow winding streets by the huge fortress of Castle
Rushen was like stepping back into the pages of history.
The castle custodians were opening the enormous wooden
doors as I walked by, and I bought a ticket and set off on a
rapid tour of one of the best-preserved seats of bygone
splendour I have ever visited. Built of local limestone and
held together with a mortar of ox blood and crushed sea
shells, its origins go back to the reign of the Vikings, and
after their demise it was extended and used as a holiday
home for a succession of absentee Lords of Man.

There are volumes of information about the occupants of
Castle Rushen, but among the reams of genealogy and
boring statistics is the touching story of Ivar the Knight,

who, in the true spirit of a romantic adventure, rescued his sweetheart Matilda from the clutches of King Reginald. According to the custom of the day, Ivar had to present his fiancée at Court to obtain the King's consent to marry, but when Reginald ran his eyes over the lovely Matilda, she stirred unkingly desires beneath his ermine cloak, and he vowed he would possess her for himself. Having a servant slip a couple of silver spoons into the pocket of the unsuspecting Ivar was all that was needed to accuse him of thieving the royal cutlery and banish him from the castle, leaving the way clear for the King to have his evil way with the fair Matilda. But the lady firmly resisted his amorous advances and promises of reward for services rendered to the Crown, until finally the exasperated Reginald clapped her in solitary confinement with instructions to pass the word up if she changed her mind. Meantime poor Ivar, devastated at the loss of his sweetheart, took a vow of piety and entered the monastery of St Mary's to devote his life to prayer.

One day, while walking in the woods thinking about Matilda, Ivar came across a small cave and, crawling inside, found it was the entrance to a subterranean passage. Curious to find out where it led to, he followed it to an iron door and had managed to prise it open when suddenly a piercing scream echoed along the passage, rooting him to the spot. It was followed by another scream and cries for help, and Ivar was ready to dash for home but, plucking up courage, he crept along the passage towards a speck of light in the distance. Peering through a chink in the door he beheld his long-lost love, 'with dishevelled hair and throbbing bosom', about to succumb to the rampant Reginald. Bursting into the room, Ivar grabbed a sword lying on a table and, not particular about point of entry, rammed it into the tyrant king before he had a chance to do any permanent damage. Grasping the weeping Matilda in his arms, Ivar carried her to the shore, where there was a boat conveniently waiting to take them to safety in Ireland. They were duly married 'and passed the remainder of their days in the raptures of a generous love, heightened by mutual admiration and gratitude'.

According to legend, one of the most powerful dynasties ever to occupy Castle Rushen was founded because an English nobleman, Sir Thomas Lathom, and his lady went bird-watching on their estate in Lancashire. While observing an eagle's nest they heard a baby crying and, having sent a servant to shin up the tree, he reported that there was a baby lying in the nest. Having no male issue of their own, the Lathoms adopted the baby and in time he inherited the estate. Some observers of the time hint that the happy discovery was nothing more than a crafty piece of jiggery-pokery planned by Sir Thomas to conceal the result of an earlier indiscretion and at the same time provide him with an heir, but the credibility of that story is best left to the historians to argue over.

When the adopted son died, he left an only daughter, Isabel, who married Sir John Stanley, the first Earl of Derby, and to mark the occasion they took the Eagle and Child as the family crest. King Henry IV (1399–1415) ordered Lord Derby to look after the Isle of Man when it was seized from the rebellious Earl of Northumberland in 1403; but later made him a present of it on the condition of 'rendering to our heirs the future Kings of England, two falcons on the days of their coronation'. Not a bad rent for their own personal kingdom. The family held on to it for over 300 years until the tenth Earl died in 1736 without issue and it passed into the control of the Duke of Atholl.

Of all the Stanleys who ruled the island, James, the seventh Earl, is the one who will be long remembered – not so much for his popularity but for the events which led to the execution of the Manx folk hero William Christian, 'Illiam Dhone' (Brown William).

Almost from the day he inherited the island the Earl seems to have deprived his tenants of their ancient rights of tenure, and it caused a lot of friction between him and his Receiver-General, William Christian, who was campaigning for the House of Keys to be more representative of the people and less a puppet of the overlord.

When the Earl dashed off to help the English king fight Oliver Cromwell and was captured and executed, the

Roundheads sent a strong force to take possession of the island, but the Earl's lady locked herself in Castle Rushen and refused to leave. The troops surrounded the castle with cannon and were prepared to blast it to pieces, but William Christian persuaded the Countess to surrender in return for the safety of the household. For a few years there was comparative peace on Man, but after Cromwell's death the English throne was restored and the island returned to the Stanleys. The eighth Earl then set about rounding up all those he considered had rebelled against the Stanley family. William Christian was arrested, and though he pleaded that his intervention had saved the lives of the Countess and her family, and Castle Rushen from destruction, the Earl was not impressed. In the parish register of Kirk Malew it records that, 'Mr William Christian, Ronaldsway, Receiver General, was shot to death at Hango Hill, January 2 1663 for surrendering the keys of the garrison to Oliver Cromwell's army. He died most penitently and most courageously, prayed earnestly, made an excellent speach, and next day was buried in the chancel of Kirk Malew.'

When I climbed to the highest parapet of the castle I could see Hango Hill, a small mound of grass close to the shore on the road from Castletown to Langness. I could not help wondering if Illiam Dhone was made to walk there from Castle Rushen on that bleak January morning or if he was taken by carriage in the manner befitting a saviour of the island and champion of human rights.

Leaving the castle, I made my way to the seafront to photograph the twelfth-century building of the old Grammar School, but a sudden mist rolled in from the sea like a pall of smoke and engulfed the town in a grey haze. The transformation from a warm morning with good visibility to a thick fog was alarming, and it was easy to understand why mariners dreaded sailing close to the Isle of Man. Though the foghorn at Langness Point could be heard sounding its mournful warning, it was difficult to decide which direction it was coming from, and creeping through fog not knowing quite where the tide was taking the ship must have been a nerve-racking experience for any navigator.

Throughout time ships and the sea have played an important part in the lives of the Manx people, and Castletown has one of the most interesting maritime museums to be found anywhere. It is an Aladdin's cave of nautical bits and pieces, navigation instruments, model ships, fishing gear and masses of photographs and paintings, spread over two floors of Bridge House – once the home of George Quayle, a brilliant and resourceful eighteenth-century Castletown businessman whose contribution to sailing-boat design has never been fully acknowledged. Like many successful men of his time with a zest for adventure, Quayle took full advantage of the highly profitable smuggling activities between the Isle of Man and the mainland, and delighted in outsailing the Revenue cutters.

During the 1930s a builder working in Bridge House knocked through a wall and discovered a find that had nautical historians leaping in the air with excitement. In a hidden chamber was George Quayle's boat, the *Peggy*, complete with masts and sails, and everything on board ready to go to sea. It was the most important nautical find of the century, the only known boat of its type in existence. By some stroke of providence, Quayle's secret boathouse had been walled up, and the *Peggy* had lain there in perfect condition for over 200 years. She was a typical coastal trader of the period, a mere twenty-six feet long and schooner rigged.

It was the *Peggy* that Quayle used for his smuggling trips, landing rum, tobacco and brandy at dead of night on the remote Cumberland coast. Always looking for ways of sailing faster than the Revenue cutters, he designed a revolutionary sliding keel which could be raised or lowered, which enabled the *Peggy* to carry more sail than usual.

Not content with beating the local boats, he took on the might of the Lake Windermere yachtsmen and in August 1796 sailed the *Peggy* over to Lancashire, where, with the aid of a wagon and team of horses, he hauled the boat to

Windermere and swept the board at the sailing regattas. In a letter to his brother he could hardly conceal his mirth:

Belle Isle, 22 Aug 96

Dear Mark

I have the satisfaction to inform you of our safe arrival here, we got across the water the same night we sailed from Douglas. We got up as far as Penny Bridge with the Boats and the following day, by the assistance of the Natives got up to Newby Bridge and were decanted clean into Windermere. I should have wrote before but that a letter would not reach before our Return ... Today we dined with the Bishop and if we did not take notice of the principle People about by accepting their invitations it might breed ill Blood and Jelousie – Calm weather has prevailed for the Most Part and the Long Bolsprit and Sliding Keels has already produced strong Symptoms of Saisma among the Devotees of Fresh Water sailing. Ct. Heywood's Boat is the Second Best in the Lakes – Modesty privents me saying who bears the Bell – Their Row Boats are indifferent. I wish I had my Row Boat here – my Life to a China Orange it would beat all. Give my duty to my Father & Love to Srs & Brs and believe me to be

Yours sincerely, G. Quayle.

Sailing back to the Isle of Man, the *Peggy* was caught out in a gale, and another of Quayle's ideas saved the day. He had developed a means of rigging canvas round the boat to keep out the spray, and on his return to Castletown reported that, 'The quarter cloths were of great protection. Without them I believe we would have gone to Davy Jones's locker and without the sliding keels we could not have carried enough sail.'

I went to look at the *Peggy* and marvelled that Quayle and his crew had ventured out into the wild Irish Sea in such a tiny boat to play cat-and-mouse with the excisemen and the certainty of a hangman's noose if they were caught.

*

The museum was so absorbing that I forgot about my arrangement to meet Dave Woods at a pub near the castle and, when I looked at my watch, I realized he had been waiting for fifteen minutes.

Waiting for someone in the comfort of a pub has many advantages over standing on a draughty street corner, and when I walked in, Dave was comfortably seated behind a pint of Castletown bitter, not the least bit perturbed that I was late. We ordered bar lunches, not forgetting Dave's wife Margaret, who had gone shopping, and settled back in the comfortable seats to browse over maps he had brought me, showing the footpath system on the island and the route of the Millennium Way. The meal and Margaret arrived at the same time.

After lunch we climbed into Dave's car and drove round Castletown Bay to the flat, scrub-covered peninsula of Langness, and parked near the lighthouse. The fog had almost cleared, and as the sun broke through, the fog siren gave a final grunt and stopped. Dave wanted to show me a memorial to a disaster in 1853, when the crowded emigrant ship *Provider* struck Langness and not a soul was saved.

'It's here somewhere. I've seen it!' Dave assured me after we had poked about among the rocks for half an hour searching for it without success.

'Well, what does it look like?' demanded Margaret hotly. 'I haven't seen anything that looks remotely like a monument.'

'It's just a message painted on a rock. You can't miss it. Keep searching!'

So we searched, crawling over sharp rocks, slipping on seaweed, falling into gullies, until we were almost worn out. Suddenly Dave gave a loud whoop of triumph. 'I've found it!' he shouted. 'Over here.'

Painted in white letters on a flat rock by the edge of the sea was the sad epitaph 'Provider. All lost 1853.'

'How many people were on board?' asked Margaret.

'I'm not sure,' answered Dave, 'but apparently only the ship's cook and an Irishman managed to scramble ashore; they died from cold and exhaustion. The ship's cat, a ginger tom, was the only survivor, and it was given to someone in Glenmaye. There's a story that an Englishman on holiday bought it and was taking it home with him when it escaped from its basket and a week later turned up again in Glenmaye and stayed there.'

We went to look at a turf-covered mound near the lighthouse known as the potato grave. A ship carrying Irish workers to the island to help dig potatoes was lost with all hands off Langness in 1832, and though they were in calling distance of the shore, nothing could be done to save them. Thirty bodies were washed ashore and placed in a communal grave.

Margaret shuddered. 'It's eerie,' she said. 'Let's go!'

In the old days an average of one ship was lost every two weeks on the rocks of Langness, and the Manx called it *'Oaie Ny Baatyn Marroo'* – 'The graveyard of the lost ships'. Pieces of ships' timbers are still to be found wedged in crevices in the rocks.

We explored the peninsula for an hour or so, enjoying the warm sun and the tang of salt air, then the Woods had to leave for home in time to meet their children coming out of school. I declined the offer of a lift back to Castletown as I wanted to visit St Michael's Isle at Derby Haven and, waving goodbye, I followed the rocky shore along the east side of the peninsula.

In an 1862 guidebook Derby Haven is described as '... one of the finest natural harbours in the Island. The bay affords excellent anchorage for large merchant ships, and is sheltered from all winds excepting East to South East.' In almost a century and a half it has lost nothing of its beauty, but the large sailing ships are gone forever. Nowadays only yachts ride to anchor, waiting for a favourable wind to take them round Langness Point.

The harbour is a horseshoe-shaped indent in the north end of Langness peninsula, and had the retreating glaciers of the Ice Age put on an extra burst of speed and cut through the narrow strip of land that joins Langness to the Isle of Man, there would be no Derby Haven, and Langness would be an island. One enterprising Lord of Man, with an eye to making a pound or two by saving ships the dangerous passage round the Point to Castletown, joined Derby Haven and Castletown with what must be one of the shortest canals ever constructed, but surprisingly very little is known about it other than a line in a seventeenth-century account of the island which says: 'Only little small boats do go up the narrow channel from the haven into the town, and cast anchor almost under the castle walls.'

On the Langness side of Derby Haven I upset a trio of golfers by inadvertently setting up my camera tripod on a convenient flat piece of ground, which I gathered from the obscenities hurled at me was the fifth hole of Castletown golf club. A portly gent, wearing outlandish tartan plus-fours and wide-brimmed sunhat, rushed towards me brandishing a golf club.

'Damn it all, man, you've ruined our game,' he yelled. 'Look what you've done!' He waved the club in the direction of a white blob on the ground, and I realized that the stone I had kicked out of the way when I was hurrying to photograph Derby Haven was a golf ball. I was full of apologies and offered to place the ball back where it had been lying, but he ranted and raved as if the fate of the universe hung on rigidly complying with the commandments laid down in the Golfer's Creed. I was determined he was not going to spoil my day, and I walked away leaving him strutting up and down like an indignant cockerel.

'Good job you didn't tangle with him, Charles,' I heard one of his friends say. 'I do believe it's that gypsy fellow I had words with near my house.'

Squinting through the zoom lens of my camera, I recognized the pompous military type who had objected to my taking Thor and Lucy across the footbridge at Ramsey.

There is nothing to equal the tranquillity of a small island for helping to restore one's composure after brushing with aggressive, ill-mannered people, and though the tiny St Michael's Island in Derby Haven is now reached by a causeway, as I lay on a headland watching the sea rise and fall against the rocks, it felt completely detached from the world. The silent ruin of the twelfth-century chapel gives the island an atmosphere of monastic peace, but locals believe it is a peace that ends with the setting of the sun – as darkness falls the ghosts of the drowned whose bodies are buried on Langness rise and are seen walking on the shore. Screams and groans are said to come from the chapel, where pirates murdered the priest and were drowned themselves taking the loot back to their ship. The story must be very effective in keeping trespassers and courting couples off the golf course!

It seems strange that the Isle of Man, with its long history of agriculture, no longer has a native breed of pony. As long ago as 1577 efforts were being made to improve horses on the island, and anyone who kept 'a stoned Horse below the value of six shillings and eight pence or any scabbed horse or mayre' was fined heavily and the poor animal thrown over the cliffs into the sea. Nearly a century later the severe regulations seem to have had some effect, for William Blundell reported that, 'The Manx breed of horses are low and little ... a reasonably tall man needs no stirrups to ascend him; but being mounted, no man need to desire a better travelling beast ... they will plod on freely and willingly with a soft and round amble ... you have no need of spurs or switch. In enduring labour and hardness they exceed others, they will travail the whole day and night also, if they be put to it, without either meat or drink.'

It was an attempt to improve the quality of Manx horses by Charles, eighth Earl of Derby, that laid the foundation for one of the greatest horse-races in the world. In 1670 the Earl put out a notice declaring: 'Out of the good affection that I have to every of my Tennants of my Isle of Man to furnish themselves with, and thereby to have a breed of good horses there: it is my pleasure to allow the sum of five pounds yearly to bee paid out of the Revenues of the Island, to be Run for, the 18 of March: and that every person who puts in a Horse for the same shall give IX s towards the enlarging of a Plate, which the winner shall oblige himselfe to buy within a yeare, with the motto as formerly: Pro Gloria Patrae Curro. [I run for the honour of the Country.]'

The only example of the plate in existence is a two-handled silver cup dated 1701 held by the Derby family. On one side is the legend: 'To give Birth to ye Royal Sport of Horse Racing, This cup was given, run for, and won at Derby Haven.' On the other side are engraved the Three Legs of Man and a mounted jockey with the motto.

The race course was a piece of land extending rather more than a mile across the peninsula of Langness, which is about where the golf course is today.

As ever, historians give widely differing accounts. Some argue, for instance, that the first race was run on 28 July 1628. Whatever date it started, it does not seem to have been the annual event the Earl intended, for in 1687, '... with the consent and approbation of the rest of the Lord's officers and 24 Keys', Governor Heywood is reported as re-establishing it and winning the race on a bay gelding called Loggerhead. For some reason the enthusiasm for the race petered out, and nothing more is heard of it until half a century after the long line of Derby Lords of Man had ended.

The first English Derby, named after the twelfth Earl, was run at Epsom in 1780. Amidst all the glitter and excitement, the multi-million-pound racehorses, top hats and champagne that are now the Epsom Derby, it would be a safe bet with any bookmaker that, if asked, few of the racegoers would be aware that the first-ever Derby was a few scruffy ponies racing each other along the shore of Castletown Bay in the Isle of Man.

While the Derby's efforts to breed quality horses on the island may well have produced a handful capable of winning races, they did little to improve the workhorses. When the Atholls inherited the Lordship of Man, Governor Lindesay wrote to the Duke asking that a stallion be sent over to improve the strain of Manx horses: 'These are very bad being a mongrel between the small Manx horses and Irish mares which are as bad as the worst Scotch garron. If the Duke will present the Stallion it will be lent free to the better class of farmers.'

Sir George Head, on a tour of the United Kingdom in 1837, wrote: 'The perambulation of the Isle of Man is better performed ... on the back of a horse than in any other way.' Though when he hired one he might well have changed his mind: 'The animal, in fact, really was I believe the very worst of steeds then on hire in the town of Castletown, and through ill luck ... I now happened to be sitting on his back. He was a very old, narrow-backed pony, combining in a rare degree in his person, the infirmities of age, with the folly and forwardness of youth. His hoofs, lifted from the ground by an unbending knee, perpetually came into contact with the loose stones in his way; which he would kick before him to the right and left, almost with sufficient velocity to kill a sparrow.'

The Manx pony must have been very similar in size to Thor and Lucy, 'about thirteen hands high and black', and like the Fell Pony of the Lake District was descended from the sturdy Galloways of southern Scotland. For some inexplicable reason the island's native breed lost favour and towards the end of the nineteenth century became totally extinct.

I walked back to Castletown along the site of the racecourse, passing King William's College (which must have been a quiet seat of learning before Ronaldsway Airport was opened; aircraft now land and take off with noisy regularity) and the infamous mound of Hango Hill where Illiam Dhone was 'shotte to death'. With ghoulish indifference the Derbys later had the gibbet removed from the traditional place of execution and built a banqueting house on the spot to celebrate the Lord's birthday and as a grandstand for the race.

The last train from Castletown to Port St Mary was depressingly empty, and I thought I would have the carriage to myself until, as the train was drawing slowly away, the guard wrenched the door open and an old man carrying two plastic bags filled with groceries stumbled in and sank, gasping for breath, into a seat. His face was the colour of a boiled lobster but, after squirting a blast from an aspirator bottle down his throat, he perked up and within minutes was chattering away as if we were old friends. Visitors to the island from areas of Britain where it is not unusual for people to live in a house for years and hardly know the name of their neighbour might need time to get used to the frank and outspoken way the Manx sometimes greet strangers.

'Where are you going?' asked the old man.

'Port St Mary,' I replied.

'Don't know your face,' he said. 'Do you live there?'

I told him about my journey round the island with my two ponies.

'Hm,' he sniffed. 'Well, if you're going to write about us, just be careful what you say. There's too many go away with the wrong impression. One feller wrote that the Isle of Man was fifty thousand alcoholics clinging to a rock. Cheeky sod!' He rummaged in one of the plastic bags and brought out two pork pies. 'Here you are,' he said. 'Have a pie. Straight from the oven; you'll not find nicer ones anywhere on the island.'

We munched our pies in silence and watched the countryside go by as the train chugged along to Colby and stopped at the little station. No one got on or off, and with a weary wave of his green flag the guard sent the train on again to Port St Mary. The old man blew pie crumbs out of his moustache and wiped his mouth with the sleeve of his jacket.

'Hey, lad,' he said, 'you were telling me that you were collecting tales about the island. I bet you haven't heard about the three fishermen, Jack, Billy and Tommy, from Peel. They were great pals and always went out drinking together. As soon as the boat hit the quay, they'd be in the pub day and night, drinking and singing and having a good time. It went on for years, and by God they must have put some booze away between 'em.

'Well, one day Tommy ups and dies, and Jack and Billy went to the funeral to see their old mate lowered down, then it was back to the pub to drink to his memory. Tommy's family put a gravestone up, but after a while the stone started to lean a bit to one side with it being in soft ground, and to stop it falling over they strung a wire from the top of it and nailed it to a post. Well, that night Jack and Billy were in the pub as usual, and after closing time they were staggering past the churchyard when Jack looks over the wall and sees the wire fastened to the top of

Tommy's gravestone. "Hey, Billy, come and look at this," shouts Jack. "Tommy must be doin' all right, he's gone and had a phone put in!"'

I never did discover the man's name, but what a marvellous old character he was. He told one hilarious tale after another, and enough historical anecdotes to fill a book – about how the Manx people used to sail to America to work during the winter, then return home for the summer; that the Panama Canal was designed by a Manxman who spoke only Manx; and that the Manx family of Cannon were head of the Mormon sect in America. He told me a fascinating story about how in his youth he and his friends had climbed aboard a ship aground on the Calf and salvaged dozens of cases containing sewing machines before it broke up and sank.

'You'll get to love this island,' he said cheerfully when I left him at Port St Mary station, 'but watch out if you go to Sulby – they say it's on the dark side of the moon!'

A stiff breeze was shaking the trees as I walked from the station to the farm, and the cloud I had seen on the horizon from Bradda Head the previous day was slowly filling the sky: a break in the fine weather looked certain. Stopping only long enough to collect my anorak the lighthouse keeper had left at the farm and wind film into my cameras, I set off to walk to the Sound overlooking the Calf of Man. The light was ideal for taking photographs, and I felt that if I left it until the following day it might rain and the opportunity would be lost.

It was very tiring climbing up the hill from Port St Mary to Cregneish, but at the summit the reward was worth the effort. I looked down on an absolutely stunning panorama of green meadows and white cottages, reaching down to a low headland where the Calf of Man and the tiny islets of Kitterland and Thoulsa sat motionless on a mirror sea. The breeze had died and there was an uncanny stillness in the air that amplified the calls of sheep and carried the roar of surf pounding against the rocks several miles away. In the sky the evening sun was dipping rapidly towards the advancing cloud, and I rushed along the road as fast as I could go to reach the headland before the light faded. I scarcely managed to take four or five shots before the sun sank behind the cloud and the bright colours of the meadow, rocks and sea faded into tones of black and grey. In the gloom the dark rocks of Kitterland and Thoulsa lost their sea-washed innocence and reared menacingly out of the water, a grim reminder of the fate of countless ships and seamen whose bones lay scattered along the sea bed in Calf Sound.

On a level patch of grass close to the shore a plaque below a wooden cross commemorates 'An Act of Heroism by Men of this Parish in their Rescue of the Crew of the French Schooner *Jeanne St Charles* in 1858'.

While on passage to Londonderry the schooner was caught in a gale and driven onto the rocks in the Sound. The crew took to the ship's boat, but it capsized in heavy seas and all six crew were left clinging to Thoulsa Rock. Relays of men hauled two boats overland from Port St Mary to try to save the crew, but before they could be launched the Captain's thirteen-year-old brother and another boy were washed off the rock and lost. The first boat was swept past Thoulsa, but the second managed to rescue the Captain, the Mate and two crewmen. An eye-witness wrote: 'I was never prouder of my countrymen than on this trying occasion. I have witnessed many wrecks and assisted at saving lives, but never saw a crew more determined to risk all to save human lives, especially taking into account the frail and tiny boat, the bad oars, the raging sea, the fearful tide rushing through the narrow channel ...'

The loss of the *Jeanne St Charles* was tragic enough, but that of the brig *Lily*, which ran aground on Kitterland in a gale in December 1852, makes an even more gruesome story.

Bound for Africa from Liverpool with a crew of thirteen and a cargo of cotton goods, barrels of rum, fire-arms and sixty-one tons of gunpowder, the *Lily* was driven into the Sound and struck Kitterland. In the collision the carpenter was crushed to death under a falling mast, two of the crew were washed overboard, and two more (including the Captain) were drowned attempting to swim to the shore. The remaining crew members were rescued and taken to Port St Mary.

While the loss of the Captain and four of his crew was a dreadful tragedy, it was nothing compared with the calamity that followed. Miraculously, the *Lily* was still in one piece on the rocks, and a Lloyds agent who was responsible for the insurance of the vessel and her cargo went to the ship with a party of twenty-seven local men and two policemen to salvage the ship. Smoke was seen coming from one of the hatches, and while the party formed a bucket chain a carpenter started to cut a hole in the deck planking to pour water into the hold. As he pierced the deck, there was a tremendous explosion and the ship was blown to pieces. Not a trace of it was left, and bits of wood, iron and human bodies were scattered over the countryside as far as six miles away from the wreck. Houses were shaken in Douglas, sixteen miles away, and people rushed out into the streets in terror. Out of the thirty men who had gone to the wreck, only one survived, and what could be found of the rest was buried in a communal grave in Rushen churchyard.

It was generally believed that the fire which caused the gunpowder to explode was due to spontaneous combustion, but Lockington Marshall in his book *Calf of Man* tells an intriguing story about a man dying in America many years after the tragedy who confessed that he was responsible for the explosion. He said that he and two companions had been on board the *Lily* to steal some of the cargo and, as it was dark in the hold, had lit a candle. It was still alight when they left, and perhaps the candle had set fire to some of the cotton goods and, when the deck was ripped open and air rushed in, it ignited the gunpowder.

Manx people probably did very nicely out of cargoes and fittings 'rescued' from stranded ships, though not surprisingly very little is recorded other than the occasional advertisement in a newspaper – 'To be sold, ship's blocks, spars, sails etc.' By the time the Receiver of Wrecks and the insurance underwriters reached a remote part of the island where a ship had gone aground, there would be little left but the hull!

On 30 September 1923 the hand of Providence guided the 6,000-ton cargo boat *Clan McMaster* through dense fog and conveniently stranded her on the rocks between the Calf and Thoulsa. She was loaded with light machinery, cotton goods, 2,000 tons of coal and sewing machines. All the crew were rescued safely, but the ship eventually slid off the rocks and sank in deep water. The records show that the salvage tug *Ranger* saved some of the machinery, yet right under the noses of the crew the locals managed to spirit away a large number of cases containing sewing machines, not to mention the Captain's binoculars and the ship's compass.

'Almost everyone in Port St Mary had a new Singer sewing machine,' the old man on the train told me, 'and some cases had spare frames in them. Farmers used them for blocking gaps in the walls.'

Thinking about it, I remembered seeing a few of them on the Calf round the top of a silage tower near the farmhouse, with the name 'Singer' prominently stamped in the centre.

'But those days have finished,' he said. 'All you get from the sea now is a few plastic fish boxes!'

On my way back to Port St Mary I stopped off at Cregneish to look round the old village, preserved in its original state as an open-air museum by the Manx National Trust, to show a way of Manx life that has disappeared for ever. The old joiner's shop, weaver's house, farmstead and smithy had closed for the day but a friendly lady custodian let me have a quick look around. It was fascinating to wander in and out of the houses and workshops, and the Manx National Trust had done a very good job in giving the impression that the village was alive and that the joiner, the weaver or the blacksmith had just put their tools down and gone out for a few minutes to visit a neighbour.

It was nearly dark when I reached the farm, and I sank wearily into my sleeping-bag, with just enough energy left to light the stove and make coffee. I longed for sleep, but a strong wind piped up and flogged the canvas of the tent all night.

11

Food Poisoning
and Fortune-Telling

There was no spectacular dawn and dew-soaked fields to boost morale when I crawled bleary-eyed out of the tent the next morning. The wind was still blowing hard, and it was dull and overcast, but thankfully the rain had kept away and I enjoyed a leisurely breakfast before striking camp and loading the ponies.

Robert, Doreen and Doreen's father came out to wave me off, and I felt I was leaving old friends as I rode out of the farmyard. 'Keep along the road for a couple of miles, then turn for Colby,' Robert said. 'And come back and see us whenever you can!' Pressing my heels into Thor's side, I urged him forward and, with Lucy striding out behind, we were on our way.

The road was very busy, but I was so captivated by the superb view across Bay ny Carrickey to Langness Point that I hardly noticed the traffic whizzing by and almost missed the road to Colby. We turned onto a narrow, winding lane and enjoyed a mile or so of undisturbed peace before joining a main road leading to Colby Glen.

Before setting off on my journey, one of the many people I contacted for advice on the history of the island was John Quilliam, a Manx historian and poet, who invited me to call on him when I reached Colby. Outside Colby post office the first person I asked had no hesitation in directing me to John's house, and with the usual Manx friendliness I was plied with cups of tea and cake by Mrs Quilliam.

John talked about his boyhood days when there were

hundreds of small farms all over the island and the farmers' wives brought fresh butter, eggs and home-cured bacon into the towns on market days. 'They're all gone now,' he said sadly. 'Thriving little farms I knew as a lad are just crumbling heaps of stones in the grass.'

One of the rapidly dwindling band of islanders whose first language is Manx Gaelic, John is an authority on place-names. 'The Vikings left us with a legacy of names from their own language, but it's easy to distinguish them from the Manx,' he explained. 'Take the name "Balla" for instance, as in Ballacreggan where you stayed in Port St Mary. You'll find the map of the island is littered with the name Balla, and it's true Manx. "Balla" means "farm", and Ballacreggan is Farm Rocky, or Rocky Farm, whereas Grenaby where you stayed in the north of the island is Scandinavian for Green Farm, "Grena" – green, and "By" farm.'

'What about that strange name "Eary Ploydwell"?' I asked.

'Well, "Eary" is a shieling or summer grazing,' he said, 'but "Ploydwell" isn't Manx at all. It's a personal name, and he was probably a skilled lead-miner imported to work in the Foxdale mines. You'll often find that happening in some of the names of farms.'

While we talked, two of John's neighbours arrived, eager to discuss the arrangements for the annual parish Columb Killey, a sort of village fête, to be held the following day, so, thanking the Quilliams for their hospitality and a very useful book on Manx place-names, I continued on to the village of Ballabeg and a quiet back road that zigzagged north towards Foxdale.

Away from the busy main road I let the ponies make their own pace, and Thor's slow plod fitted in perfectly with the lovely rural landscape. Hedgerows were ablaze with hawthorn blossom and wild flowers, filling the air with a fragrance that no perfumier could ever equal and sending bumble-bees frantic as they zoomed from one flower to another gathering pollen. A young farmer mowing thistles in a field waved as we went by, and stopped his tractor to talk and admire the ponies.

'How are you getting on?' he asked. 'I read about you in the paper. It's years since I saw Fell ponies; these two look in good fettle.' Reaching into his pocket, he pulled out a few dairy nuts and shared them between Thor and Lucy. We leant on the gate and chatted, and he told me he had moved to the island from England, but had no regrets. 'The Manx are a funny lot,' he said, 'but if they take to you, they can't do enough for you, and I wouldn't live anywhere else!'

He complained bitterly about the cost of travelling on the Steam Packet Company's ships and said that it was strangling the tourist industry.

'If the cost of getting to the island isn't drastically reduced, then people will stop coming. It's as simple as that!' he exclaimed. 'At present the Government is relying on the low rate of taxation to attract money, but it's a fickle market. In the long term it will need a lot more positive thinking to stabilize the economy, and in my view we should exploit the island's autonomy to the full. It's time it stopped clinging to its former glory as the mecca for Lancashire mill workers, and the powers ought to decide if tourism is important or not. If it is, then visitors have got to feel they are going abroad when they decide to spend their holidays here. It needs all the atmosphere of going abroad, with Customs at the sea and air ports, duty-free shops and a feeling that the Isle of Man is something really different and not just an extension of England.

'My one complaint about the Manx is that they resent incomers putting forward their ideas, and they tend to forget that some of us live here because we love it just as much as they do, and not for what we can get out of it.' He gave the ponies a few more nuts, then climbed onto the tractor. 'By the time you've finished your journey, you'll be an expert on the Isle of Man,' he said, laughing. 'You'll find there's lots of conflicting interests, but all in all there aren't many places to equal it.'

The grey cloud of morning turned blacker as the afternoon progressed. By the time we reached the edge of South Barrule plantation, the sky had all the appearance of an imminent storm, and a few drops of rain splashed onto my face. Fearing the worst, I turned into the forest and followed a track between rows of conifers. It was so dark under the trees I could barely see the way ahead, but it was a relief to escape from the wind, and there was plenty of shelter if it rained.

The semi-darkness and the sound of the wind moaning through the branches made it feel very spooky, and when the trees suddenly opened into a clearing and there stood a house, it was almost like a scene from *Hansel and Gretel*. When a lady emerged and invited me in, I strove to remember what Hansel had done in the circumstances but, instead of being clapped in a cage and fattened up for dinner, I was seated at a table and plied with cakes and tea by Betty Barry and her husband Peter, the Head Forester.

Peter and his wife very kindly offered to put me up for the night but I had already arranged to stop at Eary Ploydwell, a pony-trekking centre near Foxdale. The gathering storm was drawing ever closer and, reluctantly taking my leave, I set off again through the forest and reached the trekking centre in the early evening.

Margy and Jim Lace, and their daughter Caroline, who run the centre, could not have been nicer, and when the ponies had been unloaded and turned into a paddock I was whisked into the house and fed and watered in grand style.

Jim is a keen motor-cyclist, and after dinner we talked about the Tourist Trophy races that each year attract thousands of motor-cycling enthusiasts from all over the world and which for two weeks bring the north of the island almost to a standstill. From a humble beginning in 1907, the Senior TT had risen to be the world's premier motor-cycle race, but there are signs that its heyday is over.

'The people I talk to in racing,' said Jim, 'say that the TT is dying because the course is too long. It's nearly thirty-eight miles of ordinary road, and top stars are only interested in circuit racing these days; they reckon it's safer. It will be a sad day if it stops, but without top stars competing and drawing the crowds it's difficult to see how the race can survive!'

Both Jim and Margy have Manx ancestry going back a long way, and when the conversation turned to Manx customs Margy was a fund of information and advice. She warned that it was unlucky to utter the word 'rats' and they were always referred to as 'Longtail fellows'.

Despite threatening me with stormclouds and flicking drops of water in my face when I passed his old haunt on

South Barrule the following day, the great god Manannan relented when it came to opening the sluice gates but, just to show that I was not going to have it all my own way, he ruined any prospect of photography by covering the island in a cloak of mist. I suspect he may also have cast a spell over Thor and Lucy. They were in a sullen and unco-operative mood, puffing their stomachs out each time I tried to tighten the saddle girths and walking in opposite directions when I rode out of the yard. In the confusion Lucy's saddle caught on a gatepost as she rushed by, and a nail tore a gash in one of the canvas packs. Everything had to be unloaded and the pack repaired.

Two hours later, with dire threats ringing in her ears, Lucy meekly fell in behind Thor as we made our way along a delightful lane towards Crosby. The sweet smell of new-mown hay drifted over from the mist-hung fields, and masses of red campion provided a welcome splash of colour in an otherwise dull grey landscape. The only sound was a solitary skylark, totally unconcerned about the weather and singing its heart out to let the world know how wonderful it was to be alive. I stopped to listen, and all the fury and anger that had consumed my mind over the pack-saddle incident seemed so pointless and futile.

Descending a steep hill into Crosby village, I found the way barred by a crowd of people and by ropes across the road. A friendly policeman on duty explained that a cycle race was in progress along the TT course and, if I cared to wait until the leaders had gone through, he would radio for permission to let us cross the road. Almost immediately a cry went up from the crowd, and the first three riders streaked through the village so close together that their wheels were almost touching. In a flurry of muscular legs and sweating faces, contorted with strain, they were gone, and the policeman pulled back the rope and waved us through with a broad smile.

'You're lucky it's not a motor-bike race,' he laughed as we went by. 'You'd have been stuck here all day. Quick now, there's another bunch heading this way!'

I kicked Thor into his fastest walk and we lumbered across the race course to the safety of a road that climbed out of Crosby to a Millennium Way signpost and the start of a rough track across the hills.

My wanderings had taken me to many interesting places but, apart from skirting round the side of Snaefell during my first week, I had not really explored the hills. Crosby is more or less in the centre of the island, and between there and Ballaugh in the north is a range of imposing hills criss-crossed with ancient tracks, inaccessible to motor cars and ideal for pony travel – hills with fascinating Manx names, which in the days before the Ordnance Survey drew their fine maps were the marks that guided people from place to place: Greeba Mountain – The Peak; Slieau Ruy – Red Mountain; Lhargee Ruy – Red Slope; Colden – The Top; Sartfell – Black Mountain; and Slieau Curn – McCurn's Mountain.

It was exciting to be heading into wild country and see the mists swirling about the hillside like steam from a sorcerer's kettle. Even the ponies seemed to be spurred on by the sight of the hills, and we made good progress as we clattered up a stony track to a deserted farmhouse at Braaid and beyond, on softer ground, to a steep climb up the side of Lhargee Ruy. In the mist I could hardly see more than a few yards ahead and sometimes lost the path, but on the summit of the pass between Lhargee Ruy and Colden a strong breeze obligingly carved a hole in the cloud, and I looked down through a celestial window onto the patchwork fields of West Baldwin. The mist closed in again, thicker than ever, and the ponies were soon lathered in sweat with the strain of stumbling over rocks and sliding into peat holes, but it was too chilly to stop for a rest and I pushed on across a desolate moorland hoping to find shelter.

I offered silent thanks when a large grey object loomed up ahead of us, but it turned out to be only a cairn of stones, useless for sheltering behind. But it was a good indication of our position and I was able to work out a compass course to take us safely down to a well-defined track at the foot of Slieau Moggle. Trying to keep to a compass course when walking alone in thick mist is tedious enough, but with two ponies to care for, and ever aware of the hazards of concealed holes or steep crags, it can be very worrying. I constantly had to leave the ponies and walk ahead to reconnoitre the ground and, after what seemed like hours of crawling through rocky gullies, climbing up peat hags and sliding down heathery slopes, I was very relieved when we descended below cloud level and I saw the track a few hundred yards ahead. It should have taken no more than a few minutes to reach it, but a mischievous fairy Buggane who lived in the hills was sitting on his cloud, rather bored because trouble-making was going through a slack time, and spying a foreigner with two ponies whooped with glee and promptly turned the hillside into a vast bog.

Thor and Lucy sniffed cautiously at the bog and turned away but, with only yards to go to the track, I was determined to make it and urged them on. They plunged in and splashed and floundered, and we were almost across when the Buggane reached down and pulled Thor's feet from under him, catapulting me head first into the wettest and slimiest bit of bog he could find. Freezing water seeped through my clothes, and I crawled out saturated to the skin and covered in peaty mud. Leaving me to my fate, the ponies kept going, and when I caught up with them they were grazing the heather as if nothing had happened. I wiped as much of the peat as I could off my face and clothes and hair with a handful of grass, and changed into dry clothes. Fortified with a tot of whisky from the first aid box, my numbed body soon warmed up and, swinging into the saddle, I continued on my way.

The track was wide and well-surfaced and contoured round Slieau Moggle – 'the hill of the testicles', a shapely little mound but with a name like that unlikely ever to grace the pages of the glossy brochures or be eulogized in romantic poetry. It was odd that the track ended abruptly in the middle of nowhere as if someone had started to build a road through the hills and either lost interest or run out of money, but after the fright in the bog I was grateful for a mile of solid ground and followed it down to a main road.

A couple having a picnic by the side of a smart car ignored my greeting and regarded me suspiciously when I turned the ponies into a convenient sheep pen. While I was crouched over the paraffin stove heating a pan of soup, the man came over. I looked up and smiled, but his expression was cold and hostile.

'Have you permission to camp here?' he demanded.

'I'm not camping,' I said, 'just stopping for lunch.'

'But your horses are grazing on private land,' he persisted, 'and if it was mine, I would consider sending for the police and having you removed.'

I could hardly believe my ears. It was a nice day, I was at peace with the world, and now some officious fool was spoiling it. Perhaps he was a Buggane! Slowly and deliberately I poured the soup into a mug, put the stove out, packed it into its box and leant back against the fence.

'My friend,' I said, striving to keep my temper, 'if the land is not yours, perhaps you ought to mind your own business. I'm sure the owner would not object to the ponies grazing in his sheep pen for a few minutes, but if it will make you feel better, tell me who he is and I'll contact him as soon as I reach a phone.'

The man obviously had no idea who the owner was, and stormed back to his car muttering 'Damned insolence!' I was warmed to hear his wife say, 'Serves you right, Henry. You shouldn't interfere' – and to my surprise she came to apologize for her husband's behaviour.

'Poor dear,' she said, 'he's not himself these days. We've tried jolly hard to settle here since we left Africa, but really the challenge of living on the island has gone. The people simply refuse to accept us.' She made it sound as if they were living on a desert island surrounded by unfriendly natives.

Almost from the moment I landed at Douglas my contact with the retired colonials who had chosen the island as their final watering hole had not been the happiest of experiences, and I began to wonder if it was just an unfortunate coincidence or whether they all behaved as though they belonged to a master race.

When I left the sheep pen and led Thor and Lucy across the main road to the start of a path leading up Slieau Freoaghane, the man and his wife were sitting dejectedly by their car. A sad, lonely couple, victims of their own narrow-minded, irrational and empty world.

The mist had cleared away and the ascent to a broad plateau between Slieau Freoaghane and Slieau Dhoo was a sheer delight. Never steep enough to tire the ponies and with a fine view of Tholt-y-Will reservoir at the head of Sulby Glen, the path slanted steadily up to the summit and followed a wide ridge curving round to Slieau Curn. The ponies made it clear that they would have appreciated a rest, but there was not time to linger. To the west a fresh bank of cloud was tearing towards the island, driven on by a stiff breeze that deflected upwards when it met the hills and filled the air with a strong aroma of seaweed and the taste of salt, nearly 1,200 feet above sea-level.

The weather was rapidly deteriorating, and my taking a camera out of its case was the signal for the approaching cloud to put on an extra burst of speed. As I focused on a superb aerial view of Ballaugh forest and Glen Dhoo, it suddenly faded, and I looked up to find the summit cairn barely visible only a hundred yards away. Despite the reduced visibility, the descent down the long east side of Slieau Curn was full of interest. Though steep, the path was wide and easy to find, and being on the lee side of the hill, the air was pleasantly warm. To give Lucy a respite from carrying the dead weight of the packs, I lashed one on Thor's saddle and let them make their own way while I walked behind, stopping now and then to identify wild flowers. The cloud quickly thinned, and it cleared away altogether when we had descended a few hundred feet, revealing the sprawled-out village of Ballaugh on the edge of the fertile northern plain. Dropping steeply down to a gate, the path joined a surfaced road that marked the end of one of the most enjoyable hill rides on the whole of the island.

When TT riders cross the hump-backed bridge at Ballaugh at lightning speed during the races, for a few seconds they become airborne amid the thunderous applause of the spectators, but there was no one to witness Lucy's spectacular leap over the bridge when a horse-fly stung her on her bottom. The brute had followed us all the way down the hillside and chose the moment when we were crossing the bridge to fire its dart. I was standing on the parapet at the time, about to take a photograph, when Lucy suddenly reared up like a wild mustang and bolted over the bridge, pursued by a bewildered Thor. Fortunately they ran in the right direction up a side road to Ravensdale, and I found them being patted and fed bits of chocolate by two pony-mad young girls who thought their prayers had been answered when Thor and Lucy came hurtling into view. I let them take turns riding Thor gently up and down the road while I applied first aid to Lucy's punctured rear end, and they were so thrilled they asked if they could have his hoofprint on a piece of paper. It was the first time in his life Thor had been asked to sign his autograph, but one of the girls produced a school exercise book and he duly obliged by standing on a clean page.

Margy Lace had said that the blacksmith in Ballaugh, Barry Corder, had land by his house and would probably let me camp, and sure enough he was most obliging, and his wife Janet went to a lot of trouble shunting her own ponies about to give Thor and Lucy a paddock to themselves.

I pitched the tent in the shelter of a large tree close to the edge of a river and set about making a meal of rice mixed with a packet of shrimp-flavoured noodles. It was rather tasteless, and to help the flavour I stirred in some tinned salmon pâté and heated the evil-looking mixture on the stove. Within minutes of eating it, I realized all was not well in my stomach, and I broke out in a cold sweat. Swallowing a mug of coffee made me feel worse, and I dived out of the tent and lay on the grass, being violently sick into the river. Each time I tried to stand up, the nausea swept over me again, and I was so weak I could hardly crawl to the tent. The pain in my stomach was almost unbearable, but a dose of milk of magnesia from the first aid box only made me violently sick again. When I managed to get outside, the tent, the field, the grass and the sky started to spin out of control and I passed out. When I came to, my stomach felt as if it had been kicked by a mule, but all the sickness and dizziness had gone.

An old Highland doctor once told me that sipping drops of whisky is a useful antiseptic for troubled stomachs, and having drained the last of my medicinal bottle when I fell in the bog, I felt justified in splashing my face with cold water and walking down to the village pub for treatment. The first whisky made me feel a lot better, so I bought another just to be sure, and sank back in a corner of the crowded bar listening to a trio of locals having a heated argument about the state of the economy.

'It's all right that lot in the Government attracting the wealthy come-overs to live on the island,' said the grey-haired one, 'but what they're doing is creating a two-class society here, the haves and the have-nots.'

'Be fair now,' said Leather Jacket. 'Those people have put a lot of money into their houses, and a lot of fellers who were scratching a living in building have made a fortune, and created a lot of jobs in the process.'

'Well, maybe they did,' said a young chap, 'but you haven't worked for 'em. They treat you like dirt. When I was working on a house at Maughold, the sod who owned it used to strut about all day with a glass of gin in his hand, saying I had to call him Bwana! I told him to get stuffed, and he made the boss fire me.'

A fourth man suggested that the Government should take over all the land on the island and build chalets to attract more holidaymakers.

'You must be joking!' said Leather Jacket. 'Some of the politicians are not the least bit interested in visitors. We've got the Tourist Board spending thousands of pounds of our money trying to get people to have a holiday here, yet when a feller applied to put tables with these sunshade umbrellas on Douglas prom, it was turned down because an MHK said he didn't want the island turning into a Continental-type holiday resort.'

The conversation turned to Manx Nationalism and the origin of the three legs emblem on the Manx flag.

'It's Greek!' said the grey-haired one.

'How the hell can it be Greek?' argued Leather Jacket. 'The Vikings must have brought it. The Greeks never invaded the island any more than the Romans did!'

'We were told at school the motto was Latin,' said the young lad. 'So if the Vikings brought it, how come it's Latin?'

Leather Jacket was stumped and got up to buy a round of drinks. The rest of the people in ti e bar joined in the argument, and the noise was deafening until Leather Jacket pushed through, put the tray of drinks on the table and shouted for quiet.

'I've got it!' he said, pulling a tourist leaflet out of his back pocket. 'Listen to this!' He cleared his throat and read, ' "It would be in Sicily that the Vikings, during their excursions and settlements in the Mediterranean, came into contact with the symbol. Historians believe that Alexander III of Scotland, whose son-in-law Edmund was King of Sicily at that time, adopted the symbol when he gained control of the Isle of Man at the end of the Norse period of Manx rule in 1266." ' He paused for breath and the hubbub of conversation started again, but Leather Jacket held up his hand. 'Hang about, I've not finished yet!' he shouted. The chatter died and he turned over a page. ' "The motto *Quocunque Jeceris Stabit* was added later and first appears on Manx coins of 1668. Translated" – now listen to this!' he called to a couple who were having a private argument at the back of the room – ' "Translated, the motto means 'Whichever way you throw it, it will stand" '!'

Leather Jacket dropped the leaflet onto the table and took a triumphant swig from his beer glass. A middle-aged man sitting at a table near me, and slightly tipsy, had been listening to the arguments with half-closed eyes. Pushing his chair back, he tottered to his feet.

'Rubbish!' he bellowed. 'You've got it all wrong.'

Leather Jacket scowled. 'What do you mean, I've got it all wrong?' he said. 'It's on the paper. Here, read it for yourself!' He flung the leaflet across, but the man ignored it, and it fell to the floor.

'You've got it wrong,' he repeated.

'OK. What is it then?' demanded Leather Jacket impatiently.

The crowded bar went silent, and the man swayed back and forth clutching at a table for support.

'It's easy,' he said, slurring his words and struggling to get them in the right order. 'The three legs represent the Island's economy and the mess we're in, and the motto means:

> The buggers in the House of Keys
> Have brought the island to its knees.

He let go of the table, collapsed into his chair and fell asleep. For a few seconds there was a stunned silence, then uproar as the entire room fell about in laughter.

With only a packet of crisps and two whiskies lying in my empty stomach, I returned to the tent ravenously hungry, but rather than risk another dose of food poisoning I made do with cheese and biscuits and a mug of hot chocolate. I slept undisturbed until a crowing cockerel raised me at seven in the morning.

It was overcast when I opened the tent door, but the sun was breaking through and there was every sign of its turning into a pleasant day. Barry Corder had already set off on his rounds when I called at the house to say thanks for their hospitality, and I chatted to Jane for a few minutes before continuing on up to Ravensdale and Ballaugh Forest.

A short distance from the Corders' I passed a cluster of what estate agents glowingly describe as 'Executive Villas', each with its obligatory double garage and cars to match. An attractive woman clipping the lawn of one of the largest of the houses stopped to stare at the ponies, and there was an unmistakable expression of longing on her face, as if she would give anything to have been riding with me on that beautiful warm morning. I waved, and she waved back and continued to stare enviously after us until we climbed a steep hill and were swallowed up by the wood.

A narrow stony path, choked with fern and overhung with alder, sloped steeply up through the wood, the alder giving way first to larch, then to Norway spruce, and the path gradually improving but always unrelentingly steep. Sweat poured off Thor and Lucy, but there was no place to rest until high in the forest the path levelled out in a clearing, and I stopped for half an hour to let them cool off. The cloud had gone from the sky but a heat haze helped diffuse the strength of the sun, and it was pleasantly hot without being uncomfortable.

I lay in the warm grass and marvelled that I felt remarkably fit and well after the horrible food-poisoning experience. I made a mental note to check the remaining stock of pâté at the first opportunity. I had eaten pâté almost every day for lunch throughout my journey without any ill effects, and I suspected that when I heated it with the rice it bred lots of nasty bacteria which my digestive system took exception to and, luckily for me, instantly rejected. But why it had knocked me out in the process was a mystery.

It was so peaceful in the woods that I lay still and watched goldcrests flitting from branch to branch among the conifers, squabbling over juicy fir cones. Thor dozed in the sun, oblivious of a swarm of flies buzzing round his ears, but the ever-hungry Lucy tore at the grass, swishing her tail from side to side at the flies like an angry cat.

A long column of ants heaving small twigs back to their nest through the jungle of grass found the way blocked by my legs and immediately gathered round the chief and held their own Tynwald to decide what to do. A scout was sent out, and he scurried over my right leg, dropped into the grass, climbed onto my left leg and went back to report that he had crossed a range of mountains into a hidden valley, then climbed another range of mountains and saw the ant fort in the distance.

'That's odd,' the ant chief seemed to say. 'There weren't any mountains there this morning, but never mind, chaps, just form a chain and we'll soon have this load of firewood home.'

From an elevated position on my right kneecap he directed operations while the ants lifted and pushed, heaved and pulled each tiny twig up my trouser leg and rolled it down the other side. It was a truly magnificent feat, and I spared them the ordeal of having to repeat the process at the next mountain range by moving my legs.

In the Lake District a mixture of thick grass and heather is the favourite haunt of Britain's only poisonous snake, the adder, but on the day millions of years ago when the seas rose and severed Man from the mainland all the Manx adders were visiting relatives in Cumberland, and the island has been free of snakes ever since. That, very roughly, is the scientific version, but Manx folk prefer to believe that it is thanks to St Patrick, who having banished poisonous vipers from Ireland, sailed across the Irish Sea and performed the same service to the Isle of Man.

Perhaps in his eagerness to rid the island of snakes St Patrick's incantation was more potent than he intended, for there are no badgers, moles, foxes or deer on the island either.

Lucy was most unhappy about leaving the tasty grass and showed it by walking along as slowly as possible, making my arm ache by pulling back on her lead rope. At the end of a long and weary climb we eventually reached a gate at the edge of the forest and looked out at a very different landscape. A wide expanse of heather-covered moorland stretched into the distance and seemed to rise to the summit of Snaefell, but it was an illusion. Two miles ahead the flat moorland dipped sharply into the deep gorge of Sulby Glen. The map showed a path descending into the Glen through Tholt-y-Will forest, but a large sign nailed to a gate warned that the road was closed due to excavation work.

Normally I obey signs, but knowing that authorities have an infuriating habit of leaving them in place long after the work has been completed, and faced with the alternative of a long detour, I decided to risk it. I listened intently for the roar of machinery but there was not a sound, and opening a gate I rode into the forest down a wide track flanked by tall spruce. There was lots of evidence that bulldozers and heavy machinery had been tearing into the hillside, but no apparent reason for the 'Road Closed' notice, and I was smugly telling myself how right I was about authorities leaving signs in position for no reason when, rounding a bend, I found the way barred by a pole lashed to a tree on either side of the track. A few yards beyond it there was a large gaping hole where there had once been a bridge.

Cursing under my breath at the prospect of having to return through the forest, I searched for a way round the hole, but there was none. The only possibility was to descend a fearfully steep tree-lined slope. Removing the packs and saddles, I led Lucy down first, leaving Thor to follow in her footsteps. To attempt to take Thor on his own over a dangerous obstacle is to invite disaster! He plants his feet firmly on the ground, and nothing will induce him to move an inch, yet he would follow Lucy to the ends of the earth. We reached the safety of level ground a few hundred feet below without mishap, and I returned to start the laborious task of ferrying the equipment. It took five trips to get everything down to the ponies, but though worn out, I was enormously happy to have saved a long detour.

The muddy track slanted down in a series of tight hairpin bends and at times was so steep that Thor and Lucy had great difficulty in keeping their feet, but with a final plunge we reached the floor of the glen and rested by the Sulby river. It was incredibly hot and I sat in the shade of a tree sucking an orange while the ponies rolled the sweat off their backs in the long grass and stood up to their knees in the cool water. There was not a sign of life anywhere and only the gurgling of the river broke the silence. It was a beautiful glen, and the coniferous plantation of Tholt-y-Will fitted very nicely into the natural landscape without looking in any way 'foreign'.

In the sixteenth century the Isle of Man was known as 'the treeless isle', but when the Manx Government saw the value of afforestation as a source of timber and employment for local people, a Forest Board was formed and is now the island's biggest landowner. Regrettably, bureaucrats are often stolid and unimaginative people, unable to see beyond their own limited horizons. On a holiday island with the proud slogan 'There's no island to touch it', instead of planting areas of woodland which are pleasing to the eye and giving them attractive names like 'wood' or 'forest', the Government seems quite content to permit rectangular blocks of conifers, called plantations, to spread over the face of the island like an attack of measles.

The same lack of thought was shown when a dam was built at the head of Sulby Glen, and Druidale was flooded to provide a water supply. The face of the dam was carefully covered in turf and the area flooded with the minimum impact on the environment. It is a construction which islanders can be proud of and visitors will flock to see, but though the surrounding hills and glens have romantic names, the Government celebrated the achievement by calling it 'Sulby Reservoir'. How much more appealing it would sound if tourist brochures described it as Tholt-y-Will Lake or Loch Druidale.

With only a week left before I had to return home, I was determined to climb Snaefell, the island's highest peak, and it was only three miles away. I resisted the temptation to camp by the Sulby river and set off for the wool shed at Llergyrhenny, where the family of jackdaws lived.

The ponies were in good spirits after their rest and, leaving Tholt-y-Will, we jogged steadily along a lane flanked by Douglas fir on one side and green meadows and the river on the other. The lane and the peace ended at the main motor road, and we joined a snarling convoy of cars making their way up the long climb out of the glen. Several people stopped and we obligingly posed for photographs.

I was a bit put out when two eccentric old ladies in an ancient Morris Minor pulled into a lay-by and, as I rode by, implored me to read their palms. I tried to explain that I was not a gypsy and knew absolutely nothing about palmistry, but they would not listen and kept insisting I was an astrologer they had seen on television. They stood by Thor's head refusing to let me go until I had told their fortunes, so to humour them I slid out of the saddle and grasped their gnarled hands. They looked like any other hands to me, though I noticed that neither of them wore a wedding ring or showed signs of ever having worn one. I made a risky guess that they were hopeful spinsters and told one that, if she looked hard enough, she would meet a dark handsome stranger, and the other that she should keep her eyes open for a blond Viking, with the proviso in each case that it might take some time before they appeared. It was what they were waiting to hear, and their faces shone with pleasure.

'Thank you so much,' they whispered, and returned to their Morris Minor chattering like two schoolgirls.

I felt an absolute fraud as I watched them drive away but, remembering the old saying that 'hope springs eternal', I may well have given two old ladies who confessed to being in their eighties an added zest to life. One of them had thrust a piece of paper into Thor's saddle bag, and when I unfolded it I found to my horror that it was a £5 note.

12

The Running Trade

I reached Llergyrhenny late in the afternoon and turned the ponies loose in the paddock, dumped the packs and saddles in the shed and immediately set out for Snaefell. The weather seemed perfect for photographing the views from the summit. I could also get a shot or two of the electric train on the mountain railway and, having achieved all that, I would treat myself to a large mug of tea and a ham roll or two in the summit café.

In Manx folklore, *caillaghs* – witches – often disguised themselves as mountain hares, and on my way up Snaefell there were so many hares dashing about that I fear I may well have disturbed a coven, for in revenge they cast an evil spell. It was the only logical explanation for a chain of events which started with my camera jamming as I tried to photograph a train going down the mountain. When I reached the summit, I discovered it was the last train of the day and the snack bar was locked and bolted. A thick haze surrounded the summit and there was no view, and because I was wearing only shorts and a T-shirt, the witches sent a chilly wind to moan round the deserted buildings and raise goose pimples on my ill-clad body.

The Manx say you can see six kingdoms from the summit of Snaefell: the kingdoms of England, Scotland, Ireland, Wales and Man and, if you look up, the Kingdom of Heaven. I hung around for an hour but, apart from an occasional glimpse of Laxey and South Barrule, I saw nothing, so I trudged back down the mountain very cold, bitterly disappointed and wishing the *caillaghs* a hot reception in kingdom number seven!

Arriving back at Llergyrhenny, I pulled on thick trousers and a sweater and assembled the stove to make a meal. The previous evening's gastronomic disaster had rather destroyed my appetite, but I plucked up courage and made a pan of barbecue-flavoured noodles. Whatever taste the boffins created in the laboratory rapidly faded in the pan, and it was like eating tasteless pink putty. To wash it down, I made a mug of tea, but when I swallowed a large mouthful I discovered that my stock of teabags had been soaked in paraffin from a leaking container. The taste was awful and made me retch. I tried all sorts of flavours to kill the taste, but even after an onslaught of hot chocolate, orange juice, coffee, lemon crystals, polo mints, Mars bars and throat lozenges, paraffin was still the dominant flavour, and I spent an uncomfortable night belching volatile fumes into my sleeping-bag.

At the first glimmer of dawn the jackdaws launched into one of their noisy arguments and put paid to any hope of sleep. I got dressed, made a cup of strong coffee to help dispel the lingering taste of paraffin and opened the shed door with the intention of going for a walk.

In Manx, 'Llergyrhenny' means 'Ferny Slope', but I have a feeling that the ancient sage who first gave it a name intended it to be called 'Foggy Slope', and time has distorted it. Outside the shed the mist was so thick it was as if someone had covered the island in cotton wool, and only half a dozen paces from the shed I could not see the door. An incredibly chilly wind drove me back inside, and I retreated to my sleeping-bag with a woolly balaclava pulled over my ears to deaden the incessant cackle of the jackdaws.

I woke at nine-thirty, but the fog was as thick as ever. It was the second time I had been fog-bound at Llergyrhenny.

To pass the time I emptied the contents of the packs onto the shed floor and sorted through my stock of food and spare clothes. Most of the bags of dehydrated food I had set out with were untouched, and I had a twinge of conscience about poor Lucy, who had carried the dead weight for weeks. I was not to know that on my journey round the island I would be received with the most overwhelming generosity. Heaving the bags into a corner of the shed, I coated the saddles and bridles and my boots with a thick layer of dubbin, polished the brass tank of the paraffin stove until it shone, darned a hole in a sock, cleaned the lenses of my cameras and caught up with my notes.

When I ran out of things to do, I browsed through a mud-stained photographic magazine I had found while tidying the shed. Most of the pages had been ruined by moisture, but the advertisements were hilarious. Masquerading under the disguise of photographic models, the oldest profession in the world was blatantly offering its wares. For a mere £50 shapely ladies were available for 'uninhibited posing', refreshments provided; and a teenager of gargantuan 48 DD dimensions, clad only in a pair of yellow wellies, was willing to sit astride any gentleman so inclined and beat hell out of him with a riding crop. Someone hiding behind a box number offered high prices for photographs of men in the nude or semi-nude, and I wondered if a rather out-of-focus polaroid colourprint of me standing in my Y-fronts having a wash in the Sulby river might bring in enough money to cover the cost of another journey with Thor and Lucy!

I flung the magazine back in the heap of rubbish and searched for something else to read, but there was nothing in the shed except a notice warning about sheep scab, and instructions for using a painless castrator. Bored with the Ordnance Survey map, I hunted through packs and saddlebags and coat pockets for anything readable. My wallet revealed a number of tattered receipts and a wad of vouchers, each of which entitled me to a free wine glass if I bought an enormous amount of petrol and did not mind ending up with a dozen differently shaped glasses from a dozen different petrol companies. In my coat pocket was a crumpled note from the Inland Revenue demanding a reply to their enquiry of a year ago, an exciting letter I had received from BBC Television on the morning I left to catch the boat to the island asking if I would care to take part in a documentary about the Lake District National Park, and several almost undecipherable notes I had scribbled on bits of paper while riding along.

In a saddle bag filled with spare film, a first aid kit for the ponies, and spare notebooks I came across a rolled-up plastic bag containing typed notes about the Isle of Man's connection with Whitehaven in Cumberland, and its involvement in the lucrative smuggling activities in the seventeenth and eighteenth centuries. They had been given to me by the enthusiastic curator of Whitehaven Museum, and I had completely forgotten about them. It was not quite the light reading I had been hoping for, but it helped pass the time and, with a mug of coffee and a packet of biscuits close at hand, I settled back against the shed wall.

West Cumberland is full of stories about smugglers landing on the coast and carrying kegs of rum, brandy, tobacco, silk and tea on the backs of pack-ponies to hide-outs in the Lake District mountains, but it was not until I began researching for a book about the picturesque harbour of Ravenglass that I discovered where all the contraband came from.

When Henry IV gave the Isle of Man to the Stanleys in 1405, with the title Lord of Man, it was for services to the throne of England, but in the eighteenth century the earls exploited their domain rather more zealously than the King had perhaps intended. Though still acknowledging allegiance to the Crown they cocked a snook at the authority of the English Parliament. Through their own Manx Parliament they imposed taxes which were a lot lower than in England, and the Manx people were not slow to appreciate that, as the cost of living rocketed on the mainland, there were fortunes to be made from importing goods into the island, then 'running' them across in small boats to remote beaches on the coasts of England, Scotland and Ireland. Alarmed by the loss of revenue to the Crown coffers, the English Government set up the Customs and Excise service to curb the smuggling activities, and sent

Revenue Officers to the island to stop what the Westminster Parliament considered illegal imports and, more damaging, money-spinning exports.

Not unnaturally, the Stanleys did not take very kindly to this affront to their authority, not to mention the threat to the considerable income they enjoyed from providing the English, Scots and Irish with cheap drinks and tobacco, and sent the Revenue Officers packing. However, they were astute enough not to rock the boat too hard, and agreed to impose stricter regulations, ostensibly to reduce smuggling. But since the increased import duties were still much lower than those of the mainland, the islanders were able to pay them and still manage to make a profit from the 'running trade'. By this slick move the Crown was appeased and the Stanley fortunes swelled.

In the early 1700s, when England was battling with Louis XIV, an Act of Parliament was passed prohibiting all trade with France, but James, the tenth Earl of Derby and Lord of Man, ignored it and enabled British officials to toast the success of their King with good French brandy imported from the Isle of Man as 'Spanish wine'.

The skill and daring of the Manx smugglers in their small boats was legendary, and they resorted to all manner of tricks to avoid capture. A smuggler called Quilliam was sailing to Ireland with a cargo of rum and brandy when he was chased by a Revenue cutter, which fired a shot across his bow and signalled him to stop. Quilliam ignored it and sailed on. Another shot landed closer, and Quilliam ordered his crew to go below; he remained on deck himself and turned the boat into the wind to allow the Revenue cutter to come alongside. The Captain angrily demanded to know why he had carried on when ordered to stop, and Quilliam told him that his crew had died of cholera. Horrified, the Captain ordered the cutter to sail away, and when it was out of sight Quilliam called his men on deck and sailed on to Ireland. In another incident a Manx lugger loaded with French brandy was captured by a Revenue cutter off the Scottish coast, and the Captain put one of his crew on board and took the lugger in tow. When darkness fell, the owner of the lugger, a man named

Radcliffe from Ramsey, called to his men in Manx to hoist the sail, and at the same time he threw the Revenue man overboard, cut the tow rope and escaped into the night.

Records of the Customs and Excise show that others were not so fortunate: '... at the house of John Barnes at Bowness [Cumberland] on view of the body of a Stranger ... last night the King's Cruizing Boat Stationed 'twixt Bowness and Shinburness espied two Manks boats or smuggling vessels laden with brandy and Tobacco Steering towards the English Coast to which he immediately gave chase ... Several muskets were fired indiscriminately from the Scotch side and from the Cruizer, that the two Manks boats were at length obliged to surrender ... the deceased had received two musket balls ... and in a few moments expired ...'

The main port for passenger services to and from the Isle of Man was Whitehaven on the Cumberland coast and, as the Revenue service expanded, passengers arriving from the island found that their luggage was being strictly searched by some gentleman very new in office. For a time smuggling declined until, on the death of the tenth Earl of Derby in 1736, the Lordship of Man passed to the second Duke of Atholl. A canny Scot, he took the family motto, 'Go Forth, Fortune, and Fill thy Coffers', very much to heart by reviving the flagging 'running trade' and giving a new lease of life to an earlier Act of Tynwald which protected aliens living on the island against the proceedings of creditors for debts incurred on the mainland.

Unscrupulous adventurers and fugitives from the law flocked to take advantage of the Duke's benevolence, and any attempt to change the Act received a cool reception from the Manx authorities, who argued that, 'The prosperity of the country arose from its being the residence of strangers, and that without them it would be a miserable place.' The Protection Act was hailed as a criminal's charter, and a visitor to Douglas gives a good indication of the type of people around at the time in his poem:

When Satan tried his arts in vain
The worship of our Lord to gain,
The earth (quoth he) and all is thine,
Except one spot, which must be mine.
'Tis barren, bare, and scarce a span,
By mortals called the Isle of Man.
That is a place I cannot spare,
For all my choicest friends live there.

Hundreds of little craft sailed from the island, and Cumberland was so well supplied with cheap spirits that when 4,000 gallons of brandy, seized during 1754, were offered for auction at the Customs House at Whitehaven, they hardly fetched a bid.

While the renewed smuggling activity provided the Duke with a tidy nest-egg for his retirement, he seems to have cared little for the damaging effect the undesirables were having on the lives of the islanders. Farms were abandoned and the fishing grounds neglected as men rushed to cash in on the smuggling bonanza. With plenty of money around, ale-houses and gambling dens did a roaring trade, and an observer wrote: 'The taverns are nightly filled with tradesmen; who, on the chance of a card, a die, or a billiard ball, will hazard their last farthing ... The gamester not only rushes on a precipice to his own ruin; he frequently involves the innocent therein ... he may have reduced a virtuous wife and late-flourishing family to misery ... in Douglas there are some awful monuments of this wretchedness.' A traveller on the island about the same time remarked that there were 'very pretty women on the Island when sober'.

Furious at being cheated of thousands of pounds in excise duty, the British Government introduced the Mischief Act, '... for more effectually preventing the mischiefs arising to the revenue and commerce of Great Britain and Ireland from the illicit and clandestine trade to and from the Isle of Man'. The Duke was forced to accept it, and, in 1765 in return for £70,000 compensation, he handed over the sovereignty of the island, together with the 'royalties, regalities, franchises, liberties and sea ports'.

The prosperous era of the 'running trade' was nearing its end and, though smuggling continued in a small way for a number of years, tighter controls and greater surveillance increased the risks of being caught. In 1810 an Act of Parliament imposing a penalty of a minimum of five years service in a ship of war for anyone caught smuggling on or around the island finally sent the farmers scampering back to unearth their rusty ploughs, and the fishermen to the ship's chandlers for a new herring net.

The fog had thinned considerably when I finished reading the notes and gazed out of the shed door. I was tempted to leave immediately, but it was late in the afternoon, the ponies were grazing happily and there was nothing to be gained from rushing to get away only to have to find a place to camp further up the valley.

To salve that half of my conscience which had insisted on leaving, I pulled on my boots and walked along the main road to reconnoitre the path I wanted to take the following day over the hills to West Baldwin. It was part of the Millennium Way, heading south down the centre of the island, though whoever planned the route had ensured that no four-legged animal larger than a dog would ever walk along it, for the start of the path was marked with a high wooden stile. It was very disappointing and would mean having to make a long detour along the main road. Consoling myself with the thought that the following day was a Sunday and the roads would be deserted if I made an early start, I returned to the shed and retired to my sleeping-bag.

The jackdaws did their very best to keep me awake, but a blob of cotton wool in each ear shut the noise out, and I slept deeply and had a strange dream that I was helping smugglers to unload a cargo of pâté on the Calf of Man.

13

The Deemster's Cairn and Man's Best Friend

A young lad driving a mini destroyed my theory that the road would be deserted on a Sunday morning by roaring out of the mist. The low cloud had persisted all night, and visibility was poor when we left Llergyrhenny at eight o'clock, but the near-miss was due more to the lad's girlfriend draped round his neck than his inability to see out of the windscreen. Had we been on the road and not on the grass verge, the car would have ploughed right into us. Thor's big frame shook with fear, and Lucy was so shocked that sweat dripped off her like raindrops. It took several packets of mints before order was restored, but they were both so jumpy that I felt a lot happier when an hour later we reached a signpost and joined a path leading to West Baldwin.

For a mile, round the base of Beinn-y-Phott, we stumbled through the mist until a cold but welcome wind blew in from the west and chased the clouds to the tops of the hills. The full beauty of the Baldwin valleys was spread out below, and through the binoculars I watched a lively aerial battle as two curlews swooped and dived round a marauding blackback gull to prevent his raiding their nest. The gull struck out with his vicious yellow beak and tried every aerobatic trick he could think of, but he was no match for the attacking curlews. They harassed him relentlessly until with a loud squawk of exasperation he banked steeply to one side and flew off towards the coast.

The parallel valleys of East and West Baldwin run roughly north to south a short distance inland from Douglas, and cut deep into the hills for about five miles. Each valley has its own distinctive character, though for superb scenery there is very little to choose between them. East Baldwin has the advantage of being a quiet, little-frequented cul-de-sac, bounded by steep hills, whereas West Baldwin has a motor road running through it and boasts two small forests and a large reservoir – though how much more attractive it would sound if, instead of West Baldwin reservoir it was called Injebreck Lake, after the name of the hill at the head of the valley. The two Baldwins are separated by the long spur of Carraghan mountain, a next-door neighbour of Beinn-y-Phott, and we followed a very ancient drove road called Bayr Jiarg – Red Road – down the middle of it. It was a true mountain pass and descended gently between crumbling stone walls that had witnessed the passage of Manx life for centuries.

The helpful wind that had blown the mist away increased to almost gale force, and I did not hear the sound of approaching engines until four motor-cyclists on scramble bikes hurtled past us like screaming banshees. Although they were on a mountain path, not one of them slowed down, and the ear-splitting noise sent the ponies almost berserk with fright. Thor reared up in the air and very nearly threw me out of the saddle as he fought to bolt down the road, but I eventually managed to calm him down and slid to the ground in time to see Lucy race through a gateway and gallop out of sight down the hill. When I caught up with her on Thor, she was hiding behind a wall and absolutely lathered in sweat. What I thought was going to be a quiet Sunday morning amble had turned into a nightmare for Thor and Lucy, and apart from giving them a hug and some sweets there was nothing I could do to make up for human lunacy.

The wind moderated a little as we continued on down the drove road, though it was decidedly chilly and I was glad to reach the tiny St Luke's Church at a junction where the drove road merged with a surfaced motor road leading to Baldwin village. High on a windswept hill over a mile from the village seemed an odd choice for the village church, until reading a pamphlet inside the porch I discovered that it had been built on 'the Ridge of Justice', the site where Tynwald Courts were held before the permanent site was established at St John's. The wind had dropped, and light rain started to fall as I rode away from St Luke's and crossed to East Baldwin, but it was only a shower and died away as I rode into Booilshuggel Farm.

The Caleys were delighted to see me, and Margaret hurried to put the kettle on and make tea while Philip helped me unload the ponies and turn them into one of his fields.

In the evening the threatening weather cleared away, and a bright sun warmed the fields and evaporated the rain in spirals of wispy vapour. After dinner Philip and his son Jim left in their Landrover to gather some sheep off Slieau Ree above the farm, and I went along for the ride. When we stopped at the foot of a frighteningly steep slope, I felt sure we would have to leave the vehicle and walk, but farmers are an adaptable race and have progressed from the horse and cart through a modern technology, accepting it in their stride. Philip merely engaged low gear, and the landrover climbed slowly up the side of the hill like a fly on a wall.

A flock of crows attracted Philip's attention near the top of the hill, and as we approached we could see that they had been busy tearing at the carcase of a dead sheep. Neither Philip nor Jim seemed very concerned at the loss of a sheep, and when I expressed surprise, Philip explained it was an old ewe and there was nothing they could have done for it.

'It seems a callous thing,' said Philip, 'but it always reminds me of the time when I was a lad and worked for a farmer called Jim Webster. I was out checking the sheep this particular day, and I was really worried when I found one dead. I didn't say anything to Jim, but the next day when I found another dead I had to tell him and I was scared he would blame me, but he just pulled on his pipe and said, "Ah, well, Philip, the young ones sometimes die, but the old ones have to!"'

We drove along to a gap in a fence where sheep had been

breaking through, and Philip sent his dogs to gather the strays and drive them higher up the hill. 'We'll be about half an hour taking this lot up,' he called. 'While you're here, go and look at the Deemster's Cairn. I'll bet you've never seen anything like it. Just follow that wall!'

Wondering what could be interesting about a heap of stones, I followed the wall as instructed, but though I searched there was no sign of a cairn. I was about to give up and return to the landrover when to my astonishment I saw what appeared to be a mummified body built into the wall, with arms and legs outstretched. The 'body' turned out to be white stones in the wall, but there was no plaque or anything to explain the reason for it.

'It's in memory of a Deemster who died during a blizzard,' explained Philip as we drove back to the farm. 'I think it happened during the seventeenth century, but I've got an old book about it in the house and it'll give you the full story.'

A chapter in the book told how, in 1600, a Deemster (judge) rode from his home in the north of the island to attend the trial of a young girl who faced death by hanging. He set out in a blinding snowstorm to ride over the Bayr-ny-Ree (the Royal Way) but lost his way in the deep snow and both he and his horse were found frozen to death on Slieau Ree. Somehow the girl escaped the noose, and it is said that she and her lover built a cairn on the spot where the Deemster was found. As usual, there seems to be a certain amount of academic wrangling between historians as to how the figure of a man came to be built into the wall, but the favourite theory is that the cairn of stones was used when the mountain land was enclosed during the late eighteenth century, but a family called Quine who farmed the land at the time were enlightened enough to want to preserve the memory of the Deemster's courage and immortalized him in a life-size figure built into the wall using white stones.

In the 1930s a Manxman, Henry Hanby Hay, roused his passions in a long poem about the tragic incident in a style reminiscent of William McGonagall. Ignoring tearful pleas from his wife not to set out in the storm, the Deemster declares:

> My duty is to go.
> Charged with a wild and wilful crime
> A girl in gaol is pent.
> The law demands she should be tried
> (I think she's innocent).

The Caleys very kindly invited me to stay the night in the house, and after breakfast the following morning I set off back along the road to West Baldwin. We had completed a round trip of the island, but with two more days before we were due to leave I had telephoned Margy Lace to ask if I could finish my journey at Eary Ploydwell. 'Of course you can,' she said, 'and I'll give you a lift over to East Baldwin to pick your car up.'

To celebrate the end of the journey, buntings of fleecy white cloud were strung across a blue sky. It was warm enough to ride in shirtsleeves and, with the sun on my back and Thor and Lucy jogging along at a comfortable pace, we dropped down into Baldwin village.

Philip had told me about the mysterious Chibbyr Runna river that flowed across a narrow lane about half a mile outside Baldwin. His mother had told him it was the coldest water on the island, and at one time it was used for baptisms. I followed his directions, but at Rhyne Farm we were halted by a fierce notice declaring in large letters that it was Private Property. I was studying the map to find an alternative route when a voice said: 'Are you lost?' and I turned to find a man gazing at me over a hedge.

'I am rather,' I replied. 'I'm looking for the Chibbyr Runna river, but notices like that one are not much help!'

The man spat into the hedgerow. 'I'll tell you something,' he said. 'If you ever see a sign on the island that says "Keep out" or "Private Property", you can bet your life it's owned by a come-over. It's like sticking a label on themselves. You won't find Manx folk wasting their time with such rubbish.' He pointed down a narrow cart track. 'You'll cross the Chibbyr Runna river down there. They say it's the coldest water on the island, but put your hand in it. I wouldn't drink it if I were you, or you'll have more than Manx fairies floating around in your gut. The come-overs who own the farm higher up drain their septic tank into it.'

Thanking the man for his help, I steered the ponies down the track, and it was a rider's dream: a good surface, the aroma of damp soil, hedgerows filled with all manner of wildflowers, high trees curving overhead filtering the heat of the sun and, best of all, no room for cars!

The Chibbyr Runna river was more of a shallow stream than a river, but I stuck my hand in to test the temperature as the man had suggested. Like any stream running off a mountain, it was very cold, and though I could not be certain it was the coldest on the island, it certainly was by no means the purest. The stones had a grey, slimy look about them that usually indicated sewage pollution. Thor and Lucy confirmed it by sniffing at the water and walking away.

Leaving the river, we continued on along the track, gradually leaving the cover of the trees behind and rising gently between turf walls bordering freshly mown fields. There cannot be many smells that evoke memories of warm summer days as much as the lingering sweetness of new-mown hay. One whiff and I am transported back to my childhood, when I was allowed to sit high on the top of the load of hay as two big Clydesdale horses pulled the cart back to the farm. Modern haymaking techniques and the stern-faced men of the Health and Safety Executive have put paid to that youthful fun.

Another haymaking pastime, no doubt still indulged in by farm lads, was lying in the hay with a favourite girl, and I well remember, at the age of ten, pledging my undying love to a nine-year-old beauty with long red hair and suntanned legs. I blushed with shame and ran out of the barn when she suggested we should take our clothes off. When I met her many years later on Crewe station, she weighed about sixteen stone and had had seven children.

All too soon the delightful track ended and, arriving at Crosby, we retraced our steps up the hill we had descended on our way to take the hill route to Ballaugh. It

was a long climb, and I stopped by the side of the tiny
chapel of St Ronan to let Thor and Lucy rest and nibble at
the grass verge.

The chapel was reputed to be one of the oldest on the
island, and I opened the unlocked door and stepped
inside. I have never been a religious person, but I find
great peace in remote chapels. I sat in a pew and read my
favourite piece in the Bible, which for me puts life into
perspective:

> There is a time for everything,
>   and a season for every activity under heaven!
> A time to be born and a time to die.
> A time to plant and a time to uproot,
> A time to weep and a time to dance.
> A time to love and a time to hate,
> A time for war and a time for peace.

A loud whinnying outside the chapel echoed in the
rafters, and I rushed outside to find Thor about to be
strangled by Lucy's tether rope. I had tied them to a fence
several yards apart, and how he managed to get the rope
wound round his neck will for ever remain one of a long
list of Thor's unsolved disasters. Fortunately, the only
damage done was to his dignity, though I was forced to cut
the rope to pieces to release him.

A narrow lane at the side of the chapel was blocked by a
butcher's van delivering meat to a cottage, and while I
waited for it to move, a little old man with snow-white
whiskers bustled across to look at the ponies. He
volunteered to ask the butcher to move his van, but I
assured him that I was in no hurry, and we sat on the grass
verge and chatted about his life in farming.

'I've been retired a good many years now,' he told me,
'and I'm damned glad to be out of it. Nobody's got any
pride in what they do any more.'

'Do you go away from the island very often?' I asked. He
lit his pipe and flicked the match over the wall.

'Go away from the island?' he said. 'What the hell would
I want to do that for? I'm quite happy where I am!'

'Well, surely you must have been away at some time?'

His pipe had gone out, and before replying he applied another match to it, sucked loudly on the stem and sent a column of smoke rings drifting into the air.

'Aye, I went across to Liverpool once, must have been just after the last war, but there were too many people over there for me and I came back on the next boat.'

The butcher started to back his van down the lane and, as the old man went to guide him, a lady with a dog came out of the house holding a handful of carrots.

'Thank you very much for waiting,' she said. 'I've brought these for your ponies. Will they eat them?' Her question was answered quickly by rows of horsy teeth snatching the carrots out of her hand. 'Goodness me!' she exclaimed, jumping back in alarm. 'They must be hungry!'

'Not hungry,' I said, 'just greedy!'

The carrots had vanished in a flash, and Lucy's nose was homing in on the lady's apron pocket in the hope of more until I heaved her away.

'Are you going up the lane?' the lady asked.

'Yes,' I said. 'I'm going by Archallagan Plantation.'

Her face looked sad. 'I used to go up there a lot when my dog was young,' she said. 'I'd take a thermos flask with hot water in it, tea, a cup and some sugar and milk, and maybe a bit of cake. I carried a bottle of water and a bowl for the dog, and we'd sit up there and have a picnic in the trees. He can't do it now. He's too old.' She ran a hand fondly along the dog's head and he wagged his tail. 'He can't hear me either. He's gone very deaf, and if he walks more than a yard or two he has to rest.' She sighed heavily and continued. 'The RSPCA man said he would take him away for me and bring me another one, but I'm not sure what to do. I live on my own, and I've had him a long time.'

I said the RSPCA man would be very kind to her old dog, and if she got a new one she could start going for walks again and have picnics as she used to.

She lifted the dog gently in her arms. 'I'll have to think about it,' she said quietly and, turning round, she walked slowly back into the cottage and closed the door. It made me feel quite homesick for my old Labrador who had accompanied me on the hills for years but had reached the stage where walking was an effort. Like the lady, I could not contemplate the thought of not having him around.

Feeling very depressed, I rode slowly up the hill to Archallagan Plantation, knowing that every step brought us nearer to the end of a wonderful journey. Across the valley there was a breathtaking view of the hills, and in the bright sunlight the island looked at its best.

In Margy Lace's company no one can remain miserable for long, and her cheery welcome and a mug of tea in the kitchen when I arrived at Eary Ploydwell soon brought me round.

Thor and Lucy seemed to sense that it was all over, and tore round the paddock like a pair of race horses, hardly stopping to snatch at the grass. I could not have wished for two more enjoyable companions. Lucy had often become frustrated with Thor's unexciting pace, but in a strange way they were ideally matched and were great friends.

Leaving the ponies to their play, I returned to the house for a hot bath and spent a very pleasant evening with Margy and Jim, telling them about my experiences and the people I had met on the journey. They were highly amused about the times I had been mistaken for a gypsy, and said if I pitched my tent on Douglas prom during the summer and told fortunes, I would make enough money to explore on horseback for the rest of my life.

'Don't judge all come-overs by the few you met,' said Jim, when I told him about the pompous colonials. 'Certainly some of them are a pain in the neck, but for every one of that sort there are two who are really nice people with a genuine interest in the island. They are not Manx, and never will be, but the island has a lot to thank them for.'

The effects of a hot bath and Jim's generosity with the whisky bottle made me very sleepy, and by ten o'clock I could hardly keep my eyes open and went off to bed.

14

Journey's End

Margy drove me to the shipping office in Douglas the following morning to book a passage to Heysham, and while she went shopping I explored the town.

'In 1755 Douglas was an abode of decorum and piety,' declared the Reverend William Fitzsimmons in his history of the island published in 1805. 'Wines and spirits were plentiful but were in no request. Public houses were deserted, and those who kept them starved. The people were so friendly, so peaceable, so honest, so wise, that a cause seldom went before the Deemster in a month.' This was written at about the time when smuggling was in full swing, the British Government complaining that it was losing half a million pounds a year in revenue, and according to an observer, 'The streets of Douglas were scarce passable for several weeks, on account of the hogsheads, all the warehouses in town not being able to contain their cargoes.' The pious Reverend had either read the wrong newspapers or someone was pulling his leg!

In the eighteenth century Douglas was a wild boom town and was so important to the smuggling trade that it became '... the greatest resort in the whole Island because the haven is commodious, unto which ffrenchmen and other fforaigners are use to repair'.

There was little law and order, and foreigners and Manx flocked in by the hundred to fill the drinking dens. Sewage ran in the gutters; pigs, dogs and hens wandered about the streets, and the whole besotted town was wracked with disease. At the time the Governor and the principal officers of the island lived in isolated splendour in Castletown, but the plight of Douglas could not be ignored altogether, and a law was passed ordering the householders to clean the streets, lay pavements and keep animals under control.

Sheer neglect and an easterly gale had caused the pier to collapse into the sea, taking the lighthouse with it, and though the harbour was vital to the continuing prosperity of the island and the safety of its fishing fleet, amazingly the authorities did nothing to restore it. Vessels arriving from Whitehaven had to land passengers and cargo on the rocks or transport everything ashore in small boats, but it was the fishermen who suffered most.

One evening in September 1787 about 400 boats were fishing for herring off Douglas when, at about midnight, the wind increased to gale force and the fleet ran for shelter in the harbour. In the scramble to safety a temporary lantern hanging from a pole on the ruin of the lighthouse was knocked flying and, 'In a few minutes all was horror and confusion. The darkness of the night; the raging of the sea; the vessels dashing against the rocks; and the shrieks of the women ashore; imparted such a sensation of horror, as none but a spectator can possibly conceive. When morning came, it presented an awful spectacle: the beach and rocks covered with wrecks; and a group of dead bodies floating in the harbour. In some boats whole families perished. The shore was crowded with women ... alternately weeping over corpses of father, brother and husband.'

The tragedy did little to stir the conscience of Tynwald, and five years later visitors were still complaining about the ruinous state of the pier and the need for a lighthouse. In 1814 the Manx Government repealed the Act protecting people who had settled on the island from prosecution for debts incurred on the mainland and, like rats deserting a sinking ship, they left hurriedly for safer ground.

At first it was a great financial loss to Douglas, until the

ships taking the debt-dodgers away began to return loaded
with summer visitors on a spending spree, which inspired
what may well have been the first composer of Tourist
Board superlatives to write: 'There can be little
uncertainty as to the future of this little Isle. She has just
risen from her long night of obscurity, fresh, vigorous,
and beautiful as the ocean wave, and is preparing for a
lengthened march of flourishing greatness.' The same
gentleman, however, objected to '... droves of raw
Lancashire men and women simultaneously dipping
together, the principal recreation seeming to be splashing
each other'. He recommended that gentlemen should
wear bathing dresses similar to those worn by ladies, '...
and in order to prevent mistakes, the dresses of the
gentlemen should be of one colour, while those of the
ladies be of another ... some neutral person presiding over
the solemnities, and distributing to each their proper
covering ... There are two or three elderly gentlemen
resident in the town, who have been what is called rather
gay in early life, and whose candle is now well nigh burnt
out, to whom this office might be very judiciously
entrusted.'

Douglas grew rapidly into a very smart town of hotels,
shops and guest houses and received the final seal of
respectability when the Governor, the House of Keys, the
Deemsters, the Bishop and all the little cogs who keep the
big wheel of administration turning smoothly abandoned
Castletown and moved into more prestigious quarters in
the new island capital.

It was a beautiful morning when I came out of the Sea
Terminal building, and the sunlit hotels and guest houses
curving round the dark blue water of the bay gave it a
Mediterranean flavour. The colourful horse-drawn trams
were already busy hauling loads of laughing holidaymakers along the sea front. One old horse caused a
minor disturbance when he refused to back into his traces.
A crowd gathered, eager to give advice, but the clamour
only confused the poor animal and finally the driver had
to lead him away to the stable. I spent an enjoyable hour

browsing round the narrow streets crammed with shops selling everything from kippers to candy floss.

Walking past the Government Building, I discovered to my delight that a session of the House of Keys was about to start and, having signed my name and stated the purpose of my visit in the visitors' book, I was allowed to take a seat in the public gallery. The oak-panelled room, lined with portraits of former Speakers, was more like the Council Chamber of a prosperous city than a Parliament, but the proceedings were conducted with all the pomp and ceremony befitting a ruling legislature. Under the watchful eye of the Speaker, Sir Charles Kerruish, members presented their proposals, which were discussed and argued about in depth, and though an occasional flash of polite venom was evident, there was none of the hullabaloo and verbal abuse which Westminster politicians delight in. Like any system it probably has its weaknesses, but it is not difficult to understand why the Isle of Man Government has survived for over a thousand years and is envied throughout the civilized world.

When the session was over, I chatted to Mr Percy Radcliffe, one of the members of the House of Keys, and asked him why the island was against the party system of politics.

'Well,' he said, 'if you knew some of our members, you would say they were Tories or Socialists or Liberals, but in the house we're against the party political system for the simple reason that each party must at some time or other come up with a good idea, but if you are in opposition, no matter how good the idea is, it's your job to oppose it and hammer it, whereas in our system of government I can get up and move a resolution myself to, say, encourage another thirty thousand people to come to live on the island. It would be debated in Tynwald, everybody has a say on it, how it's going to affect hospitals, social security, education, would it create extra employment and so on. It would be voted on according to how it would benefit the island and not a political party. I would hate to see party politics come to the island myself. What we have has proved successful. People earn money, and we let them keep as much of it as possible. It's going reasonably well, and I'm happy to stick to it.'

Leaving the Government Building I walked down to the steamer pier to photograph the Tower of Refuge perched on Conister Rock just outside the harbour entrance. On the promenade a motor coach was loading passengers for an excursion. 'Take a trip round the island, sir,' the driver said as I passed by. 'See all the beauty spots!' I wanted to reply, 'I could show you a few!' but I smiled and said, 'No, thanks.'

Of the many thousands of people who dig into their pockets each year to support the work of the Royal National Lifeboat Institution, not many will have heard of Sir William Hilary, who founded it and campaigned to improve sea rescue services round the coasts of Britain. He lived in a house overlooking Douglas harbour and often acted as coxswain of the local lifeboat. In November 1830, in a dramatic attempt to rescue the crew of the Royal Mail Steam Packet *St George*, which had run aground in heavy seas on Conister, the lifeboat was flung against the ship's side, smashing her rudder and six of the ten oars. Sir William, who broke several ribs in the collision, was washed overboard with three others, but they were grabbed and hauled back on board. The lifeboat had a crew of eighteen, but somehow they managed to squeeze an extra twenty-two aboard from the *St George* and cast off for the shore.

Following the *St George* incident, Sir William suggested that Conister Rock should have a shelter for marooned seamen, and he and his wife donated almost half the £255 it cost to build the Tower of Refuge. Fortunately for the Douglas waterfront, Sir William seems to have had a regard for the visual impact of his tower, and the Douglas firm of Hansom & Welch – whose other claim to fame was the Hansom cab – designed an unusual castellated building of two small round towers, backed by a larger round tower and an even larger square tower. The idea was to give the structure a constantly changing appearance when viewed from different angles, and the architects of the hideous modern tower blocks which have destroyed the skyline of many UK cities could learn something from it.

Sir William would have been very proud of the modern fifty-foot lifeboat swinging gently on its mooring in the harbour. Many thousands of lives have been saved by the lifeboat service and, in his memory and to support the work of the RNLI, I dropped my illicit £5 fortune-telling fee into an appeal box at the Sea Terminal. I am sure the elderly ladies in the Morris Minor would have approved!

Margy picked me up by the Government Building, and a few miles outside Douglas on the way to East Baldwin to collect my horsebox and car she turned off the road into a farmyard.

'You can't leave the island without meeting Frank Christian,' she said. 'He has an amazing gift for breaking in wild horses, and people bring them to him from as far away as Ireland.'

A tall, powerfully built man, dressed in blue jeans, check shirt and a Stetson hat, was leading a large chestnut horse round the cobbled yard when we parked in front of the house, and he motioned to us to stay where we were. At the sight of the car, the horse reared up and flailed at the man with its front legs, but he dodged neatly out of the way like a boxer, all the time speaking to the horse in a quiet, unhurried voice, until to my amazement it stopped careering about and stood quite still. He stroked its neck, slowly working down and along its spine, then with a quick move he sprang onto its back. Anticipating an instant explosion of crazed horseflesh, I almost ran for the safety of the house porch, but nothing happened! The horse never flinched, and with gentle words of encouragement the man rode it several times round the yard and out into a field.

'It's incredible,' said Margy. 'That horse nearly killed someone in Ireland but it's so valuable the owner sent it over to Frank. When it arrived, no one could get near it.'

When he returned from the field, Frank talked about some of the difficult horses he had handled over many years – and in the course of training them he had broken nearly every bone in his body. He said that horses had been his life almost from the day he was born, and as a small boy he used to win the local show-jumping events riding without either a saddle or bridle, but was eventually banned because the judges said it was a stunt. 'Really it was because I won too often,' said Frank with a grin, 'but the rules have been tightened up since those days.' He could not explain the talent he had for breaking in horses. 'It's something you're born with,' he said. 'It's a gift. As long as I can remember, I've been able to get horses to trust me, and that's what breaking in is all about.'

Despite his skill and cowboy clothes, there was nothing brash about Frank. He talked in a quiet, unassuming way and was not the slightest bit affected by his reputation.

'He's an amazing character, isn't he?' said Margy as we drove away from the farm.

'He certainly is,' I said, 'and the irony of it is that true horsemen like him never make the headlines, whereas anyone who can afford to splash out thousands of pounds on a top show-jumping horse can sit on it and be carried to glory.'

Dawn was just breaking when I led Thor and Lucy out of the paddock and fastened them snugly in the horsebox for the long journey home. Margy bustled round the kitchen, making sure I had a good breakfast before setting off, and as the first rays of the sun slanted across the fields I waved goodbye to Margy and Jim for the last time and drove through the quiet countryside to Douglas.

As the ship pulled slowly away from the harbour, I felt like an exile leaving home. There is no island in the British Isles to equal this one and, like the best things in life, it has to be experienced to be truly appreciated. It is neither England, Scotland, Ireland nor Wales:

It is Ellan Vannin – the Isle of Man.